S0-BNW-202

TAG

TAG

A Diabetic
Food System

Mary Joan Oexmann, M.S., R.D.

William Morrow and Company, Inc./New York

Copyright © 1989 by Mary Joan Oexmann

Before beginning this or any other medical or nutritional regimen, consult a nutrition-oriented physician to be sure it is medically appropriate for you.

The information in this book is not intended to replace medical advice. Any medical questions, general or specific, should be addressed to your physician.

All rights reserved. No part of this book may be reproduced or utilized in any form or by any means, electronic or mechanical, including photocopying, recording or by any information storage and retrieval system, without permission in writing from the Publisher. Inquiries should be addressed to Permissions Department, William Morrow and Company, Inc., 105 Madison Ave., New York, N.Y. 10016.

Library of Congress Cataloging-in-Publication Data
Oexmann, Mary Joan.
   TAG: a diabetic food system.
   Includes index.
   1. Diabetes—Diet therapy. 2. Diabetes—Nutritional
aspects. 3. Food—Sugar content—Tables. 4. Food
exchange lists. I. Title.
RC662.038   1989   616.4′620654   88-36227
ISBN 0-688-08458-3

Printed in the United States of America

First Edition

1 2 3 4 5 6 7 8 9 10

BOOK DESIGN BY MANUELA PAUL

Preface

For many years I have cared for infants, children, adolescents, and young adults with insulin-dependent diabetes. Children and their parents have much to cope with when the diagnosis of diabetes is made. Psychologically, it is devastating to learn that life depends on insulin injections. Coping with insulin injections is difficult. The stress is further increased by restricting food.

Particularly during times of growth, energy needs are great. It is critical for children and growing adolescents to have adequate calories for normal growth and development. Insulin is a hormone that allows body cells to utilize food for energy. Without insulin, blood glucose is elevated while body cells starve. Insulin permits glucose to enter body cells.

Emphasis is placed on normalizing blood glucose to achieve metabolic control. Usually, when blood glucose is out of control, lipids or blood fats are elevated. This may well be a factor in heart and blood vessel disease, one of the complications of poorly controlled diabetes. To minimize this risk, metabolic control can be achieved by balancing food, insulin, and exercise.

Understanding the food-insulin connection is essential. Total Available Glucose (TAG) is a dietary food system that enables a person to relate their personal insulin needs directly with food. All foods are assigned values that reflect the impact of the specific food on blood glucose. Foods that have a higher TAG value have the greatest impact on blood glucose. This makes it possible to set priorities in food selection.

For most families, food selection is pleasurable. Our favorite family recipes reflect our culture and ethnic background. We express our uniqueness through food. Food is frequently used as a gift to our friends. When food is restricted we become frustrated and depressed. Rather than enjoying food, we fear it. Interpreting food labels adds to our frustration as we discover that virtually all foods contain carbohydrate.

By using this book, you will discover that insulin needs are related to the TAG in the diet. It is possible to achieve improved metabolic control. You can even work in dietary treats for special occasions without feeling as if you are cheating on your diet. Appropriate amounts of extra insulin can be calculated to cover extra food. You do not have to be left with the feeling of being either "on" or "off" the diet. You can be in charge because food decisions are based on knowing precisely what you eat and understanding its impact on blood glucose.

It takes time to learn the TAG food system. Food composition is complicated. It takes time to develop the skills to portion foods accurately. The benefit will be to achieve consistency in balancing food and insulin. Those willing to take the time to learn the TAG food system will be able to take control over their lives. Consistency is achieved because the food system offers increased flexibility. Individuals again take control of their food selection.

All people need to make food decisions centered around a well-balanced diet. This includes being aware of the need to reduce total fat and cholesterol in the diet in addition to achieving an appropriate body weight. A diet instruction of simply "Don't eat sugar" is not enough. *TAG: A Diabetic Food System* will offer answers to many of your questions about nutrition for health.

Acknowledgments

My mother, Joan Oexmann, taught me to be optimistic, value life, pay attention to detail, and have a sense of humor. Teaching and writing about Total Available Glucose (TAG) has required those characteristics.

My understanding of nutrition began at the University of Kentucky. I thank Dr. Joseph R. Fordham, who directed my graduate thesis on the effect of carbohydrate source on fat synthesis. Dr. José M. Concon, Dr. Linda Chen, Dr. Leonard V. Packett, and Dr. Abby Marlatt set the example of being generous with education and information.

Dr. Thomas Gaffney, chairman of the Department of Clinical Pharmacology, hired me in 1974 to design the nutritional aspects for the General Clinical Research Center at the Medical University of South Carolina. Dr. Norman Bell has been the director of the research unit for many years. It is through my job that I have taught many people how to improve health through modifying food decisions.

Dr. Hulda Wohltmann has set the example in caring for people who have diabetes. She emphasizes the importance of being able to directly relate food and insulin while being sensitive to the needs of the individual. TAG is for the special people who have diabetes.

TAG is based on theory but is designed for people. Ron Voegeli is one special person who has shared with me the challenge of making food decisions for health. I feel like I have been in his and his family's shoes trying to make the changes that are so important for his health. His enthusiasm as illustrated through his success has reminded me that listening is the first step to teaching. I'm lucky. I thank all of my patients.

Jacquelyn Garris has worked with me for over ten years. She, as well as Carolyn Poole, Vivian King, and Janie Bone, have been supportive throughout the writing of this book. I greatly appreciate their objectivity and honesty. All of the people working in the General Clinical Research Center have been enthusiastic.

Bill Adler, my agent, more than encouraged me to write this first book by identifying William Morrow and Company, Inc., as the best publishers. It is very exciting to have Randy Ladenheim-Gil as editor. I consider it a privilege to play a part in making information available to many.

Thanks to Jack Pickett, my husband, who cooks dinner and buys chocolate. Thanks to Lucifer the cat who purrs on top of the computer. They help me to keep my sense of humor.

Contents

Introduction

You have just learned that you or a family member has diabetes. It is a confusing time. Everything you have ever eaten seems wrong. Changes that seem so natural to the health care provider interfere with your life. It is time for a food solution.

Total Available Glucose (TAG) is a food system used by people with diabetes. It has also been used as a dietary tool for people with low blood sugar, and for weight reduction. It is suitable for anyone who would like to consume a predictable amount of glucose from foods throughout the day.

It is common for a person to be presented with a "diet sheet" during the peak of anxiety over accepting the fact of having an illness. Perhaps it is the first time that you have been sick. What you eat, how much you eat, and when you eat have always been important, but now these factors take on new significance as you begin to balance food, insulin, and exercise.

The goal of this food system is to provide your body with a predictable amount of sugar. The sugar from food is based on the composition of each food. Food selection includes the many foods that you and your family are already eating. Changes in food selection, preparation, portions, and timing will promote health for all family members.

Food decisions are complex because food is complex. It takes time to study what happens when you eat food. Balancing what and when you eat with insulin and exercise will be frustrating at times. This book provides the information needed to make food decisions for health. The reward is that you may postpone many of the health problems that occur when blood sugars vary over time.

The fear of how to live your life around diabetes will change to how to get on with your life by making healthful food decisions. It is my hope that you will be able to use TAG as a key to leading a normal life. Confidence will increase as you master the food system. Information will allow you to be "in control."

Changing what and when you eat is not simple. The challenge will be to understand the relationship between what you eat and blood sugar control. The food system is very flexible to match your lifestyle. What, when, and how much you eat is complicated, but TAG can be a food solution. There are many decisions that personalize the dietary system.

Foods are assigned TAG values based on the amount of sugar derived from that food. The TAG value reflects the impact of individual foods on blood sugar.

By the time you read and apply the information in this book, you will be on your way to becoming a nutritionist. This is not surprising, as nutrition is the study of what we eat and how our body uses food. Our children are becoming more educated in the area of nutrition by reading food labels. My hope is that you will apply the information learned here to make sense of the challenge of achieving normal blood sugars.

Consult your doctor, dietitian, and/or nurse-educator when making changes in your diet. They will be pleased to provide guidance and support as you actively make smart food decisions!

Diabetes

The symptoms of fatigue, thirst, frequent urination, weight loss, and blurred vision may take you to the doctor, where you learn you have diabetes.

Diabetes is a health problem where the ability to use food for energy is decreased. It occurs when the organ known as the pancreas fails to produce enough of the hormone insulin. A major function of insulin is to transport the body's fuel (glucose) from the bloodstream into the cells where it can then be used for energy. With diabetes, the glucose surrounds the body cells but can't get in. Rather than supplying energy, the glucose from the food you eat spills into the urine.

Twelve million Americans have diabetes. Of this number, 10 percent have Type I diabetes, while 90 percent have Type II diabetes. Type I diabetes usually occurs before age 25 but may occur at any age. Insulin replacement by injection is essential to reduce blood glucose to a normal level.

The pancreas is made of specialized tissue called the islets of Langerhans. This tissue has alpha and beta cells. The beta cells of the islets of Langerhans produce insulin. Over 80 percent of the people who are diagnosed with insulin-dependent diabetes have antibodies to the beta cells. It is an autoimmune response that decreases the ability of the beta cells to produce insulin that can be used by the body. The tendency to produce the antibodies frequently occurs in families. Viral infections have also been implicated in the destruction of the beta cells.

Type II diabetes usually occurs later in life. Weight reduction, oral medicines that stimulate the pancreas to secrete insulin, and exercise are frequent forms of treatment. The pancreas of people with Type II diabetes may change from producing too much insulin to not producing enough. When this happens, insulin replacement may be required to reduce blood glucose to a normal level.

Eighty percent of people with Type II diabetes are overweight. In the United States, fifty million men and sixty million women are overweight by 2.3 billion pounds! An alternative to obesity is to adjust food habits now. It is very hard to lose weight and keep it off without deciding to eat less sugar, eat less fat, and exercise more for life.

It takes time and effort to learn how to control blood glucose. Life is improved by incorporating healthful food decisions, exercising, and monitoring blood glucose control. Good health becomes a life pattern.

People with diabetes can monitor their success at balancing food, insulin, and exercise by measuring blood and urine glucose. Blood glucose lets you know what your blood glucose is at a specific moment in time. The blood glucose should be about 80–120 mg/ml before eating. Urine glucose tests reflect blood glucose for several hours. Your doctor will measure a substance in your blood called hemoglobin AIC. This measurement reflects blood glucose for several weeks. Exercise, food, and insulin treatment may be modified based on the combination of these measurements.

Diabetes is the number-one cause of kidney disease and blindness in the United States. It is our nation's third cause of death after heart disease and cancer. Progressive damage occurs to nerves, tiny capillaries, and major blood vessels. Heart disease, stroke, and loss of limbs may occur. The most effective treatment for the long-term complications of diabetes is prevention. This includes normalizing blood glucose through insulin replacement, food, and exercise.

Tables, Tables, and More Tables

Numbers are the language of precision. Precision leads to flexibility. Throughout this book you will find many tables. There are lots of numbers! Take one deep breath and think about how you use "numbers" all the time. Money is a meaningful use of numbers. If you can count money, you can count TAG.

Total Available Glucose has evolved through a series of many calculations. The numbers are easy to read in tables. This is fine and dandy for those people who are comfortable using numbers. In teaching nutrition, I learned that many students have number phobias. "What do I have to memorize to pass the test?" Students had to learn that numbers are the way to relate information.

Tables are used to organize information. The table of contents in this book gives you an overview of the topics to be covered. Through a number system, you find page numbers that correspond with specific information. I want information about food to be easy to find.

A table helps you find specific information. The weather table found in the daily newspaper is one of my favorite tables. The high and low temperatures are reported for specific cities throughout the country and world. The list of cities is alphabetized so that you can rapidly find the temperature of a specific place.

When you determine your meal plan you will be tempted to glance over the sequence of tables because you want the information now. But determining your meal plan is a step-by-step process in which you take information from one table to the next table. There are specific questions about height, gender, and activity that lead to finding your energy or calorie requirement. With that information, you answer questions about meal size and milk preferences, to form the personalized meal plan. There are literally thousands of options!

You will be consulting the lengthy food tables in the back of the book to find specific information about foods quickly. Study the format carefully so that you can find the information you need to select foods and determine portions. You will readily be able to compare foods.

An understanding of percentage will be helpful. This can be related to money. A quarter is 25 percent of a dollar, while a dime is 10 percent.

Reading tables, addition, and subtraction are the main arithmatic skills required to use the food system. You do not have to become a mathematician to make food decisions.

Total Available Glucose

Total Available Glucose (TAG) is a precise food system designed to provide the body with a predictable amount of glucose from foods. The food system is best suited for people with diabetes. TAG offers a direct way to relate what you eat to insulin. Increased flexibility is possible as there is a clear food-insulin connection. This will help you achieve normal blood glucose.

Food supplies your body with energy or calories in the form of protein, carbohydrate, fat, and alcohol. Protein, which supplies the body with 4 calories per gram, is found in milk, meats, eggs, fish, poultry, and grains. Protein is made up of small units called amino acids. Some of these amino acids go to the liver and are converted into glucose. Fifty-eight percent of protein is converted to glucose.

Carbohydrate, which also supplies the body with 4 calories per gram, is found in breads, grains, fruits, vegetables, cereals, and milk. All carbohydrate (100 percent) is converted to glucose in the body. Fat, which supplies the body with 9 calories per gram, is found in margarine, oils, butter, and fatty meats. Baked products and fried foods also contain fat. Fat is made of fatty acids and glycerol. Glycerol, or 10 percent of fat, is converted to glucose in the body.

In the 1920s, Dr. Rollin Turner Woodyatt proposed that the

amount of glucose from food equals the sum of the portions of protein, carbohydrate, and fat which are converted to glucose in the body. Therefore, foods are assigned TAG values based on the sum of 58 percent of the protein, 100 percent of the carbohydrate, and 10 percent of the fat. He proposed the TAG formula in an effort to provide a direct method for relating food to insulin.

During the introduction of insulin, major changes in diet were taking place for the person with diabetes. Diets changed from high fat and high alcohol to high carbohydrate. A food system which predicts the amount of glucose to be derived from foods was necessary to reduce the highs and lows in blood glucose experienced when balancing food, insulin, and exercise.

The TAG food system can be used as a total meal plan or as an adjunct. The system is very useful when deviations in the normal dietary routine are being made. Frequently, people vary food intake on holidays. The person with diabetes can safely do this if the amount of insulin taken matches the food intake.

The TAG food system can also be used when food intake is reduced during illness or when coping with the varied food intake of toddlers.

The emphasis is to closely match insulin with food. This is especially useful for people who wear a device that supplies insulin to the body in very small but frequent amounts throughout the day. This devise is called an insulin pump. The food system offers increased flexibility through precision.

A 2000-calorie diet contains 100 grams of protein, 225 grams of carbohydrate, and 80 grams of fat. This equals 291 TAG. This diet has a calorie distribution of 20 percent protein, 45 percent carbohydrate, and 35 percent fat.

100 grams protein	×	58%	=	58 TAG
225 grams carbohydrate	×	100%	=	225 TAG
80 grams fat	×	10%	=	+ 8 TAG
		Total	=	291 TAG

When TAG is used as a total meal plan, foods are placed into the categories of meat, milk, starch, sugar, and fat. The food groups assure a suitable protein, carbohydrate, and fat distribution. The food system becomes a combination of counting and exchanging.

The amount of glucose from food (TAG) can be easily calculated from the protein, carbohydrate, and fat content of each food. This leads to increased variety in both food selection and portions. My hope is to help you improve blood glucose control through providing a food system leading to increased flexibility. It is easier to understand the relationship between what you eat and blood glucose. People with diabetes actively participate in the food-decision process.

Weighing Foods

Accurate food portioning is fundamental to the success of the Total Available Glucose food system. The food decision process includes the selection, preparation, portioning, and timing of foods throughout the day. Accuracy makes it possible for all of the food decisions to work together. This is particularly important for the person who has diabetes.

The fastest way to portion foods accurately is through weighing foods. Using the household measurements of cups and tablespoons is suitable for recipes, but both messy and time-consuming when assembling an individual meal. This is because you have to transfer food from the serving dish to the measuring device to the plate. This allows time for the food to get cold. Also, washing dishes may be fun for some but I would rather be painting than washing the dishes!

As you look through the food tables, you will notice that measurements for common portions are listed. It is important to start with the familiar measurements of cups, teaspoons, and tablespoons. As you progress, you will become familiar with the weights of foods (ounces and grams).

Consider the following example to understand the pros and cons of measuring and weighing foods. Seeing is believing. Measure ½ cup of water (4 ounces = 120 grams) and ½ cup of sugar (3½ ounces = 100 grams). Addition tells you that two ½ cups equal a whole cup. The weight is the sum of 120 grams and 100 grams or 220 grams. Well, guess what. The sugar goes into solution and those two ½-cup measurements end up being less than ¾ cup! So much for 8 ounces equals a cup. A cup of the sugar solution weighs 10 ounces! You may be wondering what to do with this sugar solution containing 100 grams of sugar. It is the recipe for hummingbird feeders.

Measuring versus weighing food is unpredictable for many items. Twelve people measured 2 tablespoons of raisins. The measured portions weighed 21–41 grams (25 ± 5). Each of us is different when it comes to measuring fruits and vegetables.

The shape and size of the food item will change the amount of food that will fit into a measuring cup. A cup of finely chopped nuts will weigh more than a cup of pecan halves. Some of the space in the cup of pecan halves is displaced by air. A cup of diced carrots weighs more than a cup of sliced carrots for the same reason. It is common for the portioning of fruits and vegetables to vary. The variation is particularly important for the foods that are high in TAG.

The "small," "medium," and "large" portions vary from person to person. Twenty-four people selected a "medium"-size potato from a box of twenty-eight potatoes weighing 180–300 grams (230 ± 30). There was a two-fold difference in the weight of the selected potato! It's interesting to note that the larger the person, the larger the potato. The same confusion in portion size occurs with apples, bananas, oranges, peaches, and pears. Also, patients have told me that the medium-size portion varies. "A medium-size banana? It depends on how hungry I am!"

Weighing of foods eliminates the confusion of household measurements and arbitrary portion sizes. Weighing food is accurate and reproducible. Scales which weigh up to 500 grams (a little more than a pound) can be purchased from restaurant supply and kitchen shops for about twenty-five dollars. Scales weighing up to 500 grams are the the most convenient, as you can weigh the food directly onto the plate. You can weigh the foods as quickly as the time it takes to serve them.

Food portions are frequently compromised by rounding off

food amounts to ounces. This is particularly important when weighing high-carbohydrate foods. For example, consider the following portions of corn or cereal rounded off to the nearest ounce. Approximately 30 grams equal 1 ounce.

Corn	Rounded Off	
20 grams	= 1 ounce	= 4 TAG
30 grams	= 1 ounce	= 6 TAG
40 grams	= 1 ounce	= 9 TAG

Cornflakes		
20 grams	= 1 ounce	= 18 TAG
30 grams	= 1 ounce	= 27 TAG
40 grams	= 1 ounce	= 36 TAG

People usually feel uncomfortable weighing foods in grams for the first time. It is unfamiliar. Start with things you know. How many times have you tried to decide if a letter needed one or two stamps? You need one stamp if the letter weighs less than 30 grams. You need two stamps if the letter weighs more than 30 grams but less than 60 grams.

Take a few minutes to find a stack of nickels and two flashlight batteries. Your hands work very well for learning to estimate the weight of foods. Compare foods to the weight of a nickel (5 grams) and a size-D battery (80 grams).

margarine, a pat	= 1 nickel	= 5 grams
crackers, a two-pack	= 1–2 nickels	= 5–10 grams
cheese, one slice	= 4 nickels	= 20 grams
bread, one slice	= 5 nickels	= 25 grams
egg, jumbo size	= 1 D battery	= 80 grams
tangerine	= 1 D battery	= 80 grams
banana	= 2 D batteries	= 160 grams

The weight of many items is stated on the container. Reading labels is very helpful in learning portions:

1 pound = 454 grams; 1 ounce = 28.5 grams

How much does a stick of margarine weigh? Four sticks to a pound. One stick weighs $454 \div 4$ or about 114 grams. Compare the weight of a size-D battery (80 grams) plus seven nickels (35 grams) to a stick of margarine. It weighs the same. Margarine is all fat so a stick of margarine contains only 11 TAG but 1000 calories!

Is one stamp enough postage? You need two stamps if the letter weighs more than six nickels.

Set priorities when deciding which foods need to be weighed with the greatest precision. The foods that are highest in TAG or highest in calories require the greatest care. A typical meal might contain the following portions of food. The amount of TAG in a gram of the food is also shown.

Dinner				*TAG/grams*
chicken	82 grams	=	15 TAG	0.18
mixed vegetables	100 grams	=	13 TAG	0.13
potato, frozen	85 grams	=	22 TAG	0.26
chocolate candy	28 grams	=	19 TAG	0.65
dinner roll	28 grams	=	17 TAG	0.56
2%-fat milk	101 grams	=	7 TAG	0.07
	Total	=	93 TAG	

The chocolate candy contains 0.65 TAG per gram. It will need to be weighed with much more care than the serving of mixed vegetables which contains only 0.13 TAG per gram.

STEPS TO USING A SCALE

	(1) Empty Scale	(2) Scale and Container	(3) Turn Dial to "0"	(4) Food into Container
Food Platform				
Pointer	at "0"	at "100"	at "0"	at "200" food weighs 200 grams

The TAG Value of Foods

There are many food solutions to health problems. Many people choose to ignore the relationship between what they eat and what happens to their body. Many people do not choose to be overweight, but deny the relationship between the food they eat and their weight and state of health. That is not a healthful food solution.

If you have diabetes, you may want to simplify your diet and eat exactly the same thing each day. It is true that the consistency will help control your blood glucose. Boring! Good health requires a variety of foods for you to consume essential minerals and vitamins. One choice is to learn your TAG requirement and the TAG value of foods.

Foods contain protein, carbohydrate, and fat, which turn to glucose in the body. The amount of glucose to be derived from protein is 58 percent. The amount of glucose derived from carbohydrate is 100 percent. The amount of glucose derived from fat is 10 percent. TAG equals the sum of the parts of protein, carbohydrate, and fat that turn to glucose in the body.

TAG = 58% protein + 100% carbohydrate + 10% fat

The calculations in this book are based on this formula. However, it is very reasonable for you to simplify the formula.

Rounding off 58 percent to 60 percent will not significantly compromise your calculation. It will make it more rapid.

TAG = 60% protein + 100% carbohydrate + 10% fat

If you know the protein, carbohydrate, and fat content of a food, you can know its TAG value. Calculating the TAG value of foods is fun when you first learn how to do it. It gives you a different way of looking at food. You can think of the TAG value of the food as an amount reflecting impact on blood glucose. A food with a high TAG value will increase your blood glucose more than a food with a low TAG value.

If you are a nutritionist, you can really get into the numbers and come up with long lists of foods, as you will find in the food tables in the back of the book. Playing this number game is great for a nutritionist. As you will be able to tell from the many tables in this book, I think in numbers. However, it is unfair for you to have to become a nutritionist just because you have diabetes! So, the calculations have been done for you.

The food tables at the back of the book list over four hundred foods. Breads, cereals, fruits, vegetables, meats, dairy products, and fats are listed in those food tables. Also, information on foods used in baking is provided in the chapter on recipes and the TAG and calorie contents of fast-foods, frozen dinners, and infant foods are in the chapter on convenience foods. Use the index to find specific foods. You will be able to consult the tables to easily find the TAG value of foods frequently consumed. However, you will probably also think of many foods that are not listed. This is not surprising when you consider the very large number of foods on the market. Also, new foods and food combinations are continually introduced. To increase your variety, learn to calculate TAG accurately.

How many TAG are in a "Big Mac"? A "Big Mac" contains 26 grams of protein, 39 grams of carbohydrate, and 31 grams of fat.

60%	×	26 grams of protein	=	16 TAG
100%	×	39 grams of carbohydrate	=	39 TAG
10%	×	31 grams of fat	=	+ _3 TAG_
		Total	=	58 TAG

How many TAG are in a food containing 30 grams of protein, 80 grams of carbohydrate, and 20 grams of fat?

60%	×	30 grams of protein	=	_____ TAG
100%	×	80 grams of carbohydrate	=	_____ TAG
10%	×	20 grams of fat	=	+ _____ TAG
		Total	=	_____ TAG

Answers:

60%	×	30 grams of protein	=	18 TAG
100%	×	80 grams of carbohydrate	=	80 TAG
10%	×	20 grams of fat	=	+ _2 TAG_
		Total	=	100 TAG

How did you do? For practice, go to the kitchen and look at food labels providing information on the protein, carbohydrate, and fat content. I just went to the kitchen and found a box of "Fiber One" made by General Mills: 1 ounce (30 grams) of cereal provides 2 grams of protein, 23 grams of carbohydrate, and 1 gram of fat.

60%	×	2 grams of protein	=	1 TAG
100%	×	23 grams of carbohydrate	=	23 TAG
10%	×	1 gram of fat	=	+ _0 TAG_
		Total	=	24 TAG

This looks straightforward enough until you realize that this particular cereal is very high in fiber. Fiber is a type of carbohydrate that is not absorbed by the body. It will not become TAG! Reading the box closer, I find that 13 of the 23 grams of carbohydrate are fiber. The cereal contains $23 - 13 = 10$ grams of usable carbohydrate. One ounce of cereal provides only 11 TAG.

60%	×	2 grams of protein	=	1 TAG
100%	×	10 grams of carbohydrate	=	10 TAG
10%	×	1 gram of fat	=	+ 0 TAG
		Total	=	11 TAG

There are times when people find TAG difficult because it is a different way of counting food intake. You may have counted both calories and grams of carbohydrate in the past. The TAG system eliminates that extra counting as it includes all of the food information into a single unit which can be related to insulin. The relationship between insulin and TAG is discussed in the chapter "The Glucose-to-Insulin Ratio."

Practice calculating TAG by reading labels of the foods you frequently eat.

Consider the TAG value of some frequently consumed foods. The numbers have been rounded off.

⅔-cup of green beans	=	4 TAG
1 egg	=	5 TAG
1 slice of bread	=	13 TAG
1 cup of milk	=	17 TAG
1 medium orange	=	17 TAG
2.1-ounce Milky Way	=	46 TAG

Using TAG, it is easy to tell which foods will increase your blood glucose the most. A Milky Way would increase your blood glucose almost ten times more than one egg!

You will be able to use the food tables to determine the amount of TAG in common portions. The weights of the portions are listed in both ounces and grams. When I instruct people about diet, I always hear a cringe at the word "grams." I suppose you can't really hear a cringe, but if you could, that is the reaction to anything unfamiliar. Remember that an American nickel weighs five grams. One ounce equals about six nickels (30 cents) or about 30 grams.

Fixed food portions are one of the most frustrating aspects of a food system. It doesn't matter who you are or what your nutritional needs are, most people with diabetes are told that they must have three fruits each day. The amount is specified. No more, no less. It is a little bit like a world where everyone must wear a size-6 shoe!

The Kentucky Derby is run on the first Saturday in May. I was brought up in Kentucky so I know that beautiful roses are in bloom then. Also, my grandmother always told me that it is the day for strawberries to be ripe. I don't know if it is always true, but it does remind me that many foods are seasonal. TAG offers you a way to have more strawberries without feeling as if you are "off your diet."

You can easily calculate the TAG of all portions of food by multiplying the weight of the food in grams times TAG/gram. If you choose, multiply the weight of the food in ounces times TAG/ounce. Calculating the TAG value of foods increases flexibility in selecting food portions.

$$\text{TAG} = \text{Weight in grams} \times \text{TAG/gram}$$
$$\text{TAG} = \text{Weight in ounces} \times \text{TAG/ounce}$$

For illustration, the weights of the common portions of the following foods are presented. The weights of common portions are listed in the first food table, "TAG and Calorie Content of Common Portions." The conversion factors are listed in the second table, "TAG Factors—Food Weights to TAG." Both food tables are in the back of the book.

Food	Weight		TAG/ounce		TAG
⅔ cup green beans	3.5 ounces	×	1.1	=	3.9
1 egg	1.7 ounces	×	2.7	=	4.6
1 slice of bread	0.8 ounces	×	16.0	=	12.8
1 cup of milk	8.6 ounces	×	2.0	=	17.2
1 medium orange	4.9 ounces	×	3.5	=	17.2
2.1-ounce Milky Way	2.1 ounces	×	21.7	=	45.6

Food	Weight		TAG/gram		TAG
⅔ cup green beans	100 grams	×	0.04	=	4.0
1 egg	48 grams	×	0.10	=	4.8
1 slice of bread	23 grams	×	0.56	=	12.9
1 cup of milk	244 grams	×	0.07	=	17.1
1 medium orange	140 grams	×	0.12	=	16.8
2.1-ounce Milky Way	60 grams	×	0.76	=	45.6

TAG/ounce and TAG/gram are numbers that are rounded off, which explains why there are minor differences between the calculated TAG values based on weight in ounces compared to grams. Don't be bothered by this. The accuracy is very high! You have doubled your accuracy by weighing versus measuring food.

The math required to use TAG is simple addition and subtraction, if you use the TAG value of common portions. If food portions vary, multiplication is the only other math skill needed. The skills needed to use TAG are reading tables to find specific information about individual foods, and adding TAG to match your TAG requirement.

Study how the TAG/gram or TAG/ounce conversion factors were used to determine the amount of TAG in the varied portions of Raisin Bran. Many people eat breakfast cereal for a snack. The "What is a bowl of cereal?" discussion frequently occurs during a dietary interview. The best way to answer the question is by asking the person to show me, by pouring the cereal into a bowl that looks like the one at home and then weighing it.

Food	Weight		TAG/gram		TAG		TAG
Raisin Bran	30 grams	×	0.87	=	26.1	=	26
Raisin Bran	45 grams	×	0.87	=	39.2	=	39
Raisin Bran	60 grams	×	0.87	=	52.2	=	52

Food	Weight		TAG/ounce		TAG		TAG
Raisin Bran	1.0 ounce	×	25.5	=	25.5	=	26
Raisin Bran	1.5 ounces	×	25.5	=	38.3	=	38
Raisin Bran	2.0 ounces	×	25.5	=	51.0	=	51

If possible, weigh foods in grams. Suppose the amount of Raisin Bran you poured into the bowl was not exactly a 1- or 2-ounce portion. You could weigh the food until it equals a precise amount. This requires more time than pouring out the portion, finding the precise weight, and multiplying by the conversion factor.

Initially, grams may seem more complicated than ounces because grams are unfamiliar. In the long run, grams will be much easier because you can always use whole numbers. When you weigh by ounces, you will have to work with fractions, which tends to make the math confusing.

10 grams	=	0.35 ounce	=	⅖ ounce
20 grams	=	0.70 ounce	=	⅘ ounce
30 grams	=	1.05 ounces	=	1 ounce
40 grams	=	1.41 ounces	=	1⅖ ounces

Information for both weights is provided to help you find what works for you. The food system is for you and it must satisfy your needs!

The best way to determine how much TAG is in a food is to identify what works best for you. There are four ways to determine the TAG value of foods. They are:

1. Use "common portions" and directly find the TAG value in the table "TAG and Calorie Content of Common Portions."

2. Weigh your food in grams and multiply it by TAG/gram found in the table "TAG Factors—Food Weights to TAG."

3. Weigh your food in ounces and multiply it by TAG/ounce found in the table "TAG Factors—Food Weights to TAG."

4. Calculate the TAG value from the protein, carbohydrate, and fat content of the food:

TAG = 60% protein + 100% carbohydrate + 10% fat

Study the following meal and determine the TAG.

Food	Weight		TAG/gram		TAG
chicken	100 grams	×	0.12	=	_____
mashed potatoes	200 grams	×	0.14	=	_____
broccoli	100 grams	×	0.08	=	_____
margarine	5 grams	×	0.10	=	_____
strawberries	120 grams	×	0.07	=	_____
roll	30 grams	×	0.60	=	+ _____
			Total	=	_____

Answers:

Food	Weight		TAG/gram		TAG
chicken	100 grams	×	0.12	=	12.0
mashed potatoes	200 grams	×	0.14	=	28.0
broccoli	100 grams	×	0.08	=	8.0
margarine	5 grams	×	0.10	=	0.5
strawberries	120 grams	×	0.07	=	8.4
roll	30 grams	×	0.60	=	+ 18.0
			Total	=	74.9 TAG

The meal TAG can be rounded off to 75 TAG.

It is important to know the answer to the next question as it will help you set priorities on what foods will influence your blood sugar the most.

What food has the highest TAG value? _____

What food has the lowest TAG value? _____

What would the TAG value of the meal be if you decided to have 60 grams (2 ounces) of ice milk? (By consulting the food tables you'll find that ice milk contains 0.25 TAG/gram or 7.1 TAG/ounce.) _____

Answers:

Mashed potatoes have the highest TAG, while margarine has the lowest TAG.

60 grams of ice milk contains 15 TAG. The meal with ice milk contains 90 TAG (75 + 15 = 90 TAG).

How much TAG did you have for breakfast? You probably did not weigh your breakfast this morning, so estimate the amount by adding the TAG value of common food portions.

Name of Food	Amount	TAG
_____	_____	_____
_____	_____	_____
_____	_____	_____
_____	_____	_____
_____	_____	_____
_____	_____	_____

There are times when you might want to know how much food is equal to a specific TAG. The food table that provides the TAG/gram and TAG/ounce also provides the grams of food equal to specific TAG amounts. When you first look at this table (page 137), the quantity of numbers seem overwhelming. With practice, this table offers incredible flexibility in relating food portions to TAG. The table reads like a mileage map. On the left is the name of the food item. The numbers are food portions in grams that are equal to a specific amount of TAG.

Most people dread division. It is harder than addition and subtraction. You will be able to use this table easily to determine a specific food portion equal to a specific amount of TAG. For example, if you needed 16 TAG of milk, the portion would be 232 grams. One TAG equals 10 percent of 10 TAG. Two TAG equals 10 percent of 20 TAG. Three TAG equals 10 percent of 30 TAG.

Grams of Food Equal to TAG

Food item	5	10	15	20	25	30
2%-fat milk	72	145	217	289	362	434

2%-fat milk:		
72 grams	=	5 TAG
145 grams	=	10 TAG
217 grams	=	15 TAG
289 grams	=	20 TAG
362 grams	=	25 TAG
434 grams	=	30 TAG

What portion of milk contains 16 TAG?

15 TAG			=	217 grams
+ 1 TAG	=	10% of 145 grams	=	+ 15 grams
16 TAG			=	232 grams

What portion of milk contains 18 TAG?

20 TAG			=	289 grams
− 2 TAG	=	10% of 289 grams	=	− 29 grams
18 TAG			=	260 grams

What portion of milk contains 24 TAG?

25 TAG			=	362 grams
− 1 TAG	=	10% of 145 grams	=	− 15 grams
24 TAG			=	347 grams

Grams of Food Equal to TAG

Food item	5	10	15	20	25	30
Cheerios	6	13	19	25	31	38

Cheerios:			
	6 grams	=	5 TAG
	13 grams	=	10 TAG
	19 grams	=	15 TAG
	25 grams	=	20 TAG
	31 grams	=	25 TAG
	38 grams	=	30 TAG

What portion of Cheerios contains 30 TAG? _____ grams
What portion of Cheerios contains 26 TAG?

25 TAG			=	_____ grams
+ 1 TAG	=	10% of _____ grams	=	_____ grams
26 TAG			=	_____ grams

What portion of Cheerios contains 19 TAG?

Answers:
38 grams of Cheerios contains 30 TAG.
32 grams of Cheerios contains 26 TAG.

25 TAG			=	31 grams
+ 1 TAG	=	10% of 13 grams	=	+ 1 grams
26 TAG			=	32 grams

24 grams of Cheerios contains 19 TAG.

20 TAG			=	25 grams
− 1 TAG	=	10% of 13 grams	= −	1 grams
19 TAG			=	24 grams

If you were going to have Cheerios and milk for breakfast and needed to have 60 TAG, what portions would you use? There are many answers to this question that work.

___ TAG	=	milk	=	___ grams
+ ___ TAG	=	Cheerios	=	___ grams
60 TAG				

Study the food table to begin to learn the TAG amounts of the foods that you frequently eat.

The Meal Plan: 20% Protein, 45% Carbohydrate, 35% Fat

The meal plan is based on your calorie and schedule needs. A primary goal of the meal plan is to provide consistency in Total Available Glucose so that insulin requirements can be balanced with food. This will help you achieve normal blood sugars throughout the day. The meal plan is met by selecting from a large variety of foods. The variety will lead to satisfying nutrient requirements.

One method of determining your pattern is to match the TAG of the diet you are currently consuming. If you are starting anew, you can follow this chapter in a stepwise fashion and determine your TAG requirements.

The step-by-step process includes determining your:

1. calorie requirement

2. meal and snack size

3. calorie source (% protein, % carbohydrate, and % fat)

4. TAG requirement

5. milk preference

6. TAG distribution among the food groups of meat, milk, starch, sugar, and fat.

Designing the meal plan may seem complicated. However, if you follow the example, you will be able to construct a meal plan that is truly personalized. Sample meal plans are also provided.

1. Calorie Requirement

A calorie is a unit of heat or energy that comes from food. Calories are the fuel for your body to work. If you eat more calories than you need, you gain weight. If you eat fewer calories, you lose weight. Age, sex, height, weight, and activity all influence your calorie requirement. The following table provides a starting point to determine your calorie requirement. The numbers are based on sex, height, recommended weights, an age of thirty years, and light, moderate, or heavy activity. If you are younger than twenty-five years, add 100 calories to the stated amount. If you are older than thirty-five years, subtract 100 calories from the stated amount. The numbers are estimates. Consult your doctor, dietitian, and/or nurse educator to determine the calorie requirement that is best for you!

When you first discover that you have diabetes, you may be eating large amounts of food and losing weight. Insulin makes it possible for your body to use the food that you eat. Therefore, when you start taking insulin, you will probably need to eat less food.

Our example, Lucy, is a 5' 7" woman of moderate activity. She requires 1800 calories to maintain her weight. If Lucy needed to reduce her weight, she could decrease her calories by 500 per day to achieve a weight loss of 1 pound per week. Her calorie requirement would be 1300 calories per day: $1800 - 500 = 1300$ calories.

Calorie Requirements for Women

Height*	Pounds*	Low	Activity Medium	High
4'9"	114	1400	1600	1700
4'10"	115	1400	1600	1700
4'11"	117	1500	1600	1700
5'0"	120	1500	1600	1800
5'1"	123	1500	1600	1800
5'2"	125	1500	1700	1800
5'3"	130	1500	1700	1800
5'4"	133	1600	1700	1900
5'5"	137	1600	1700	1900
5'6"	140	1600	1800	1900
5'7"	144	1600	1800	1900
5'8"	147	1700	1800	2000
5'9"	149	1700	1800	2000
5'10"	152	1700	1800	2000
5'11"	155	1700	1900	2000

Calorie Requirements for Men

Height*	Pounds*	Low	Activity Medium	High
5'1"	134	1800	2000	2100
5'2"	137	1800	2000	2200
5'3"	139	1900	2000	2200
5'4"	142	1900	2100	2200
5'5"	145	1900	2100	2300
5'6"	148	2000	2100	2300
5'7"	151	2000	2200	2400
5'8"	154	2000	2200	2400

*Height and weight without shoes or clothing.

Calorie Requirements for Men

Height*	Pounds*	Low	Activity Medium	High
5'9"	157	2100	2300	2500
5'10"	160	2100	2300	2500
5'11"	164	2200	2400	2600
6'0"	167	2200	2400	2600
6'1"	171	2200	2400	2700
6'2"	175	2300	2500	2700
6'3"	180	2300	2600	2800

*Height and weight without shoes or clothing.

Weights are adapted from the 1983 Metropolitan Height and Weight Tables for Men and Women. The original tables were published by the Metropolitan Life Foundation in the *Statistical Bulletin,* Vol. 64, No. 1, January–June 1983. The weight is suitable for a person with an average frame. Consult your doctor to determine the weight that is best for you.

2. Meal and Snack Size

Lucy requires 1800 calories to keep her weight constant. She likes a fast, easy, and small breakfast totaling 25 percent of her food for the day. She works, and likes to pack a medium-size lunch of 30 percent of her food for the day. She prepares a larger hot supper comprising 35 percent of her food. She likes a small snack of 10 percent of her food for the evening.

Foods are divided throughout the day by having meal sizes of 20–25 percent and snacks of 0–20 percent. For Lucy, the food is divided 25, 30, 35, and 10 percents, for a total of 100 percent. Your total must equal 100 percent!

Personalize the meal plan to match your preferences and schedule. How would you like your meals timed throughout the day? There are many combinations that equal 100 percent. Do not skip meals. Your total must equal 100 percent!

POSSIBLE MEAL AND SNACK SIZES

						Example
Breakfast	20%	25%	(30%)	35%	=	30%
Snack	(0%)	10%	15%	20%	=	0%
Lunch	20%	25%	(30%)	35%	=	30%
Snack	(0%)	10%	15%	20%	=	0%
Supper	20%	25%	(30%)	35%	=	30%
Snack	0%	(10%)	15%	20%	=	+ 10%
				Total	=	100%
Breakfast	20%	(25%)	30%	35%	=	25%
Snack	0%	(10%)	15%	20%	=	10%
Lunch	20%	25%	(30%)	35%	=	30%
Snack	(0%)	10%	15%	20%	=	0%
Supper	20%	(25%)	30%	35%	=	25%
Snack	0%	(10%)	15%	20%	=	+ 10%
				Total	=	100%

SELECT MEAL AND SNACK SIZE

						You	*Lucy*
Breakfast	20%	25%	30%	35%	=	_____	25%
Snack	0%	10%	15%	20%	=	_____	0%
Lunch	20%	25%	30%	35%	=	_____	30%
Snack	0%	10%	15%	20%	=	_____	0%
Supper	20%	25%	30%	35%	=	_____	35%
Snack	0%	10%	15%	20%	=	+_____	+ 10%
				Total	=	_____	100%

3. What Kind of Calories

Calories are derived from protein, carbohydrate, fat, and alcohol. Each of these nutrients provides different amounts of calories and different amounts of TAG.

Before the days of insulin, the diet for people with diabetes was very high in fat and alcohol because less insulin is required for the body to utilize these calories. With insulin, a person with diabetes can eat much larger amounts of carbohydrate. Diet histories show that the average calorie distribution of the person with diabetes is 45 percent carbohydrate, 35 percent fat, and 20 percent protein. The most recent recommendations are to increase carbohydrate, decrease fat, and decrease protein to the calorie distribution of 55 percent carbohydrate, 30 percent fat, and 15 percent protein.

Most people find it very difficult to consume the high-carbohydrate, low-fat diet. This is not particularly surprising for the person who has diabetes. For years, people have been advised not to eat starchy foods. You may have been told to simply avoid carbohydrates. That's easy to say, but you have to get your calories from somewhere!

First, consider how many calories you get from protein, carbohydrate, fat, and alcohol. Recall the amount of calories that come from each:

1 gram protein	=	4 calories
1 gram carbohydrate	=	4 calories
1 gram fat	=	9 calories
1 gram alcohol	=	7 calories

Second, consider how many grams of protein, carbohydrate, fat, and alcohol are in 100 calories.

100 calories of protein	÷	4	=	25 grams of protein
100 calories of carbohydrate	÷	4	=	25 grams of carbohydrate
100 calories of fat	÷	9	=	11 grams of fat
100 calories of alcohol	÷	7	=	14 grams of alcohol

Finally, consider how much TAG you get from 100 calories of protein, carbohydrate, fat, and alcohol.

25 grams of protein	×	58%	=	14.5 TAG
25 grams of carbohydrate	×	100%	=	25.0 TAG
11 grams of fat	×	10%	=	1.1 TAG
14 grams of alcohol	×	10%	=	1.4 TAG

When calorie source is considered, carbohydrate provides twenty-five times more TAG than fat. Fat and alcohol are both very high in calories and very low in TAG. It is not surprising that the diets before insulin were butter and booze! The calories from fat and alcohol could be used by the body with a smaller impact on blood sugar. Today, both butter and booze are considered unhealthful for all people to consume. The low-fat diet is encouraged because people with diabetes have double the risk of getting fat deposits in the walls of blood vessels (atherosclerosis).

On special occasions, you may choose to have alcohol. Moderation is advisable for everyone. If you have diabetes and take a drink, it is particularly important to have it with a meal. When you have alcohol, decrease fat in the meal. Along the line of generalities about nutrition, prepare food for family members, including the one with diabetes, at one time, using your usual cooking methods. The person with diabetes is different only in terms of having special skills in knowing food portions. There is no need for separate pots!

Food preparation illustrates the relationship between calories and TAG. Consider different ways of fixing 3½ ounces of chicken (100 grams). Breading chicken rapidly increases TAG, while frying chicken rapidly increases calories. The most effective way to reduce weight is to reduce fat.

Baked chicken	=	110 calories	=	12 TAG
Breaded baked chicken	=	155 calories	=	19 TAG
Breaded fried chicken	=	245 calories	=	20 TAG

The calorie distribution for most people with diabetes is 20 percent protein, 45 percent carbohydrate, and 35 percent fat. The calorie distribution of the average U.S. diet is 15 percent protein, 50 percent carbohydrate, and 35 percent fat. The future goal for all people is 15 percent protein, 55 percent carbohydrate, and 30 percent fat. Many people may need to reduce fat to 20 percent!

These numbers have little meaning until illustrated as food. These 600-calorie meals have the varied calorie distributions.

	Current Diabetic	Current U.S. Intake	Future For All
protein	20%	15%	15%
carbohydrate	45%	50%	55%
fat	35%	35%	30%
TAG	87	91	98
skim milk	10 ounces	7 ounces	5 ounces
orange juice	8 ounces	8 ounces	7 ounces
eggs	2	1	1
toast	2 slices	3 slices	4 slices
margarine	3 pats	4 pats	3 pats

It is best for most people with diabetes to begin with a meal plan that is close to current eating habits. Next, achieve a balance among insulin, food, and exercise. Finally, slowly make adjustments to decrease fat. Change is much easier to achieve in steps than all at once! For many people, it is quite an accomplishment to decrease fat intake to 35 percent of calories. This is not surprising when you consider that most fast-food meals provide 50 percent of calories from fat.

The next chapter is devoted to illustrating how to design a meal plan with a calorie distribution of 15 percent protein, 55 percent carbohydrate, and 30 percent fat. Our example, Lucy, has chosen a calorie distribution of 20 percent protein, 45 percent carbohydrate, and 35 percent fat.

Meal Plan Distribution	Lucy	You
	1800 Calories	_____
Breakfast	25%	_____
Snack	0%	_____
Lunch	30%	_____
Snack	0%	_____
Supper	35%	_____
Snack	+ 10%	+ _____
Total	100%	_____

4. Amount of TAG at Each Meal and Snack

You have probably noticed that there are lots of tables. It is the most efficient way for you to personalize your meal plan. Read the table the way you read the mileage table found in maps. Match the desired calorie level in the left column with the percent of food at each meal and snack. Follow along with Lucy to discover that 25 percent of the 1800 calories equals 66½ TAG, 30 percent equals 76½ TAG, 35 percent equals 92 TAG, and 10 percent equals 25 TAG. Identify how much TAG is needed to match your desired food distribution.

Lucy: 1800 calories			Your Meals: _____ calories		
Meal	%	TAG		%	TAG
Breakfast	25%	66½	Breakfast	_____	_____
Snack			Snack	_____	_____
Lunch	30%	76½	Lunch	_____	_____
Snack			Snack	_____	_____
Supper	35%	92	Supper	_____	_____
Snack	10% +	25	Snack	_____	+ _____
	Total	260 TAG		Total	_____ TAG

AMOUNT OF TAG FOR MEALS AND SNACKS
20% Protein, 45% Carbohydrate, 35% Fat

Calories	TAG	10%	15%	20%	25%	30%	35%
1000	143	15	20	30½	35½	41	51
1100	158	15	25	30½	41	46	56
1200	173½	15	25	30½	41	56	61
1300	189	20	30	35½	46	56	66½
1400	204	20	30	41	51	61	71½
1500	219½	20	35	46	56	66½	76½
1600	229½	25	35	46	56	71½	81½
1700	245	25	35	51	61	71½	86½
1800	260	25	40	51	66½	76½	92
1900	275½	30	40	56	66½	81½	97
2000	291	30	46	56	71½	86½	102
2100	306	30	46	61	76½	92	107
2200	321½	30	51	66½	81½	97	112
2300	336½	35	51	66½	86½	102	117½
2400	352	35	51	71½	86½	107	122½
2500	367½	35	56	71½	92	112	127½
2600	382½	40	56	76½	97	117½	132½
2700	388	40	61	76½	97	117½	137½
2800	403	40	61	81½	102	122½	143
2900	418½	40	61	81½	107	127½	148
3000	434	45	66½	86½	107	132½	153
3100	449	45	66½	92	112	132½	158
3200	464½	45	71½	92	117½	138	163½

5. Milk Preferences

Milk is a very nutritious food. It is a good combination of protein, carbohydrate, and fat and also supplies calcium, phosphorous, and vitamin D. Ten TAG of milk may be just the food to have when you suspect that your blood sugar is low. One of the advantages of the TAG system is that you have the flexibility to include and exclude milk as you choose. To determine the distribution of TAG among the food groups, you need to decide when you want to have milk. Two servings each day are recommended. Lucy likes to have milk at breakfast and snack. When do you want milk? One advantage to TAG is that it is very easy to change your milk decision from day to day.

Example	TAG	Milk?	Your Meals	TAG	Milk?
Breakfast	66½	yes	Breakfast	____	____
Snack			Snack	____	____
Lunch	76½	no	Lunch	____	____
Snack			Snack	____	____
Supper	92	no	Supper	____	____
Snack	+ 25	yes	Snack	+____	____
	Total 260			Total ____	

6. Distribution of TAG Among Food Groups

More tables! Use the following tables to select the meat, milk, starch, sugar, and fat combination that matches your desired TAG. Study Lucy's meal plan, which equals 1800 calories. This is the last step.

Lucy: 1800 calories

Meal	%	TAG	Meat	Milk	Starch	Sugar	Fat
Breakfast	25%	66½	10	10	35	10	1½
Lunch	30%	76½	15	0	45	15	1½
Supper	35%	92	15	0	55	20	2
Snack	10%	+ 25	+ 0	+10	+ 15	+ 0	+0
		260	40	20	150	45	5

Your Meal Plan

Meal	%	TAG	Meat	Milk	Starch	Sugar	Fat
Breakfast	——	——	——	——	——	——	——
Snack	——	——	——	——	——	——	——
Lunch	——	——	——	——	——	——	——
Snack	——	——	——	——	——	——	——
Supper	——	——	——	——	——	——	——
Snack	+——	+——	+——	+——	+——	+——	+——
Total	——	——	——	——	——	——	——

Over twenty-five hundred meal plans can be derived from these tables. If you decide to change your calorie level, meal size, distribution of calories, or milk preference, you can follow the same steps to find the meal plan that best meets your needs. My hope is to provide the flexibility for you to design a meal plan to satisfy your individual requirements.

The next chapter provides meal plans for the calorie distribution of 15 percent protein, 55 percent carbohydrate, and 30 percent fat.

MEAL PATTERN WITH MILK
20% Protein, 45% Carbohydrate, 35% Fat

TAG	Meat	Milk	Starch	Sugar	Fat	Calories
30½	5	5	20	0	½	210
35½	5	5	20	5	½	245
41	5	10	20	5	1	285
46	5	10	25	5	1	315
51	5	10	25	10	1	350
56	5	10	30	10	1	385
61	10	10	30	10	1	420
66½	10	10	35	10	1½	460
71½	10	15	35	10	1½	495
76½	10	15	40	10	1½	530

MEAL PATTERN WITH MILK
20% Protein, 45% Carbohydrate, 35% Fat

TAG	Meat	Milk	Starch	Sugar	Fat	Calories
81½	10	15	40	15	1½	560
86½	10	15	45	15	1½	595
92	10	15	50	15	2	635
97	10	15	50	20	2	670
102	10	20	50	20	2	705
107	15	20	50	20	2	740
112	15	20	55	20	2	775
117½	15	20	60	20	2½	810
122½	15	20	65	20	2½	845
127½	15	25	65	20	2½	880
132½	15	25	70	20	2½	915
137½	15	25	70	25	2½	950
138	15	25	70	25	3	950
143	15	25	75	25	3	985
148	20	25	75	25	3	1020
153	20	25	80	25	3	1055
158	20	30	80	25	3	1090
163½	20	30	85	25	3½	1130
168½	20	30	85	30	3½	1160

MEAL PATTERN WITHOUT MILK
20% Protein, 45% Carbohydrate, 35% Fat

TAG	Meat	Starch	Sugar	Fat	Calories
30½	5	25	0	½	210
35½	5	25	5	½	245
41	5	30	5	1	285
46	10	25	10	1	315
51	10	30	10	1	350
56	10	35	10	1	385
61	10	40	10	1	420
66½	10	40	15	1½	460
71½	15	40	15	1½	495

MEAL PATTERN WITHOUT MILK
20% Protein, 45% Carbohydrate, 35% Fat

TAG	Meat	Starch	Sugar	Fat	Calories
76½	15	45	15	1½	530
81½	15	50	15	1½	560
86½	15	55	15	1½	595
92	15	55	20	2	635
97	15	60	20	2	670
102	20	60	20	2	705
107	20	65	20	2	740
112	20	70	20	2	775
117½	20	70	25	2½	810
122½	20	75	25	2½	845
127½	25	75	25	2½	880
132½	25	80	25	2½	915
137½	25	85	25	2½	950
138	25	85	25	3	950
143	25	85	30	3	985
148	25	90	30	3	1020
153	30	90	30	3	1055
158	30	95	30	3	1090
163½	30	100	30	3½	1130
168½	30	100	35	3½	1165

SNACK PATTERNS

TAG	Calories	With Milk			Without Milk	
		Meat	Milk	Starch	Meat	Starch
15	105	0	15	0	0	15
20	140	0	20	0	0	20
25	175	0	10	15	5	20
30	205	0	10	20	5	25
35	240	0	15	20	5	30
40	275	0	15	25	5	35
45	310	0	15	30	5	40

SNACK PATTERNS

		With Milk			Without Milk	
TAG	Calories	Meat	Milk	Starch	Meat	Starch
50	345	0	15	35	5	45
55	380	5	15	35	10	45

MEAL PLANS
20% Protein, 45% Carbohydrate, 35% Fat
25% Breakfast, 30% Lunch, 35% Supper, 10% Snack

1000 Calories = 142½ TAG

Meal	TAG	Meat	Milk	Starch	Sugar	Fat
Breakfast	35½	5	5	20	5	½
Lunch	41	5	0	30	5	1
Supper	51	10	0	30	10	1
Snack	+ 15	0	15	0	0	0
Total	142½					

1200 Calories = 173 TAG

Meal	TAG	Meat	Milk	Starch	Sugar	Fat
Breakfast	41	5	10	20	5	1
Lunch	56	10	0	35	10	1
Supper	61	10	0	40	10	1
Snack	+ 15	0	15	0	0	0
Total	173					

1400 Calories = 203½ TAG

Meal	TAG	Meat	Milk	Starch	Sugar	Fat
Breakfast	51	5	10	25	10	1
Lunch	61	10	0	40	10	1
Supper	71½	15	0	40	15	1½
Snack	+ 20	0	20	0	0	0
Total	203½					

MEAL PLANS
20% Protein, 45% Carbohydrate, 35% Fat
25% Breakfast, 30% Lunch, 35% Supper, 10% Snack

1600 Calories = 224 TAG

Meal	TAG	Meat	Milk	Starch	Sugar	Fat
Breakfast	56	5	10	30	10	1
Lunch	66½	10	0	40	15	1½
Supper	76½	15	0	45	15	1½
Snack	+ 25	0	10	15	0	0
Total	224					

1800 Calories = 260 TAG

Meal	TAG	Meat	Milk	Starch	Sugar	Fat
Breakfast	66½	10	10	35	10	1½
Lunch	76½	15	0	45	15	1½
Supper	92	15	0	55	20	2
Snack	+ 25	0	10	15	0	0
Total	260					

MEAL PLANS
20% Protein, 45% Carbohydrate. 35% Fat
25% Breakfast, 30% Lunch, 35% Supper, 10% Snack

2000 Calories = 290 TAG

Meal	TAG	Meat	Milk	Starch	Sugar	Fat
Breakfast	71½	10	15	35	10	1½
Lunch	86½	15	0	55	15	1½
Supper	102	20	0	60	20	2
Snack	+ 30	0	10	20	0	0
Total	290					

2200 Calories = 320½ TAG

Meal	TAG	Meat	Milk	Starch	Sugar	Fat
Breakfast	81½	10	15	40	15	1½
Lunch	97	15	0	60	20	2
Supper	112	20	0	70	20	2
Snack	+ 30	0	10	20	0	0
Total	320½					

2400 Calories = 352 TAG

Meal	TAG	Meat	Milk	Starch	Sugar	Fat
Breakfast	86½	10	15	45	15	1½
Lunch	107	20	0	65	20	2
Supper	122½	20	0	75	25	2½
Snack	+ 35	0	15	20	0	0
Total	351					

2600 Calories = 382½ TAG

Meal	TAG	Meat	Milk	Starch	Sugar	Fat
Breakfast	97	10	15	50	20	2
Lunch	117½	20	0	70	25	2½
Supper	132½	25	0	80	25	2½
Snack	+ 40	0	15	25	0	0
Total	387					

2800 Calories = 407½ TAG

Meal	TAG	Meat	Milk	Starch	Sugar	Fat
Breakfast	102	10	20	50	20	2
Lunch	122½	20	0	75	25	2½
Supper	143	25	0	85	30	3
Snack	+ 40	0	15	25	0	0
Total	407½					

MEAL PLANS
20% Protein, 45% Carbohydrate, 35% Fat
25% Breakfast, 30% Lunch, 35% Supper, 10% Snack

3000 Calories = 437½ TAG

Meal	TAG	Meat	Milk	Starch	Sugar	Fat
Breakfast	107	15	20	50	20	2
Lunch	132½	25	0	80	25	2½
Supper	153	30	0	90	30	3
Snack	+ 45	0	15	30	0	0
Total	437½					

3200 Calories = 464 TAG

Meal	TAG	Meat	Milk	Starch	Sugar	Fat
Breakfast	117½	15	20	60	20	2½
Lunch	138	25	0	85	25	3
Supper	163½	30	0	100	30	3½
Snack	+ 45	0	15	30	0	0
Total	464					

The Meal Plan: 15% Protein, 55% Carbohydrate, 30% Fat

Most people need to decrease fat in their diet. Replace the calories from fat with carbohydrate. It is difficult to accomplish a dietary distribution of only 30 percent fat. But there are many individual meals where a very low fat intake can be achieved. However, recognize that it is very easy to consume much more fat. "Eating out" a couple of times each week can greatly increase the fat in your diet.

It is common for a fast-food meal to provide 50 percent of the calories from fat. Be realistic. Successful change is a gradual process. Frying foods is not a good idea for every meal but is all right from time to time. Make small changes over time. Let the TAG food system be a flexible tool to provide a predictable amount of glucose.

1. Calorie Requirement

Match your sex, height, and activity level to determine your calorie requirement.

Calorie Requirements for Women

Height*	Pounds*	Low	Activity Medium	High
4'9"	114	1400	1600	1700
4'10"	115	1400	1600	1700
4'11"	117	1500	1600	1700
5'0"	120	1500	1600	1800
5'1"	123	1500	1600	1800
5'2"	125	1500	1700	1800
5'3"	130	1500	1700	1800
5'4"	133	1600	1700	1900
5'5"	137	1600	1700	1900
5'6"	140	1600	1800	1900
5'7"	144	1600	1800	1900
5'8"	147	1700	1800	2000
5'9"	149	1700	1800	2000
5'10"	152	1700	1800	2000
5'11"	155	1700	1900	2000

Calorie Requirements for Men

Height*	Pounds*	Low	Activity Medium	High
5'1"	134	1800	2000	2100
5'2"	137	1800	2000	2200
5'3"	139	1900	2000	2200
5'4"	142	1900	2100	2200
5'5"	145	1900	2100	2300
5'6"	148	2000	2100	2300
5'7"	151	2000	2200	2400
5'8"	154	2000	2200	2400
5'9"	157	2100	2300	2500
5'10"	160	2100	2300	2500

*Height and weight without shoes or clothing.

Calorie Requirements for Men

Height*	Pounds*	Low	Activity Medium	High
5'11"	164	2200	2400	2600
6'0"	167	2200	2400	2600
6'1"	171	2200	2400	2700
6'2"	175	2300	2500	2700
6'3"	180	2300	2600	2800

*Height and weight without shoes or clothing.

Weights are adapted from the 1983 Metropolitan Height and Weight Tables for Men and Women. The original tables were published by the Metropolitan Life Foundation in the *Statistical Bulletin*, Vol. 64, No. 1, January–June 1983. The weight is suitable for a person with an average frame. Consult your doctor to determine the weight that is best for you.

2. Meal and Snack Size

The possible meal sizes vary from 20 to 25 percent of your total TAG. The possible snack sizes vary from 0 to 20 percent of your total TAG. Your total must equal 100 percent.

POSSIBLE MEAL AND SNACK SIZES

						Example
Breakfast	20%	25%	(30%)	35%	=	30%
Snack	(0%)	10%	15%	20%	=	0%
Lunch	20%	25%	(30%)	35%	=	30%
Snack	(0%)	10%	15%	20%	=	0%
Supper	20%	25%	(30%)	35%	=	30%
Snack	0%	(10%)	15%	20%	=	+ 10%
				Total	=	100%

POSSIBLE MEAL AND SNACK SIZES

						Example
Breakfast	20%	(25%)	30%	35%	=	25%
Snack	0%	(10%)	15%	20%	=	10%
Lunch	20%	25%	(30%)	35%	=	30%
Snack	(0%)	10%	15%	20%	=	0%
Supper	20%	(25%)	30%	35%	=	25%
Snack	0%	(10%)	15%	20%	=	+ 10%
				Total	=	100%

SELECT MEAL AND SNACK SIZE

						You	Lucy
Breakfast	20%	25%	30%	35%	=	____	25%
Snack	0%	10%	15%	20%	=	____	0%
Lunch	20%	25%	30%	35%	=	____	30%
Snack	0%	10%	15%	20%	=	____	0%
Supper	20%	25%	30%	35%	=	____	35%
Snack	0%	10%	15%	20%	=	+____	+ 10%
				Total	=	____	100%

3. What Kind of Calories

If you use the tables from this chapter, the calorie distribution will be 15 percent protein, 55 percent carbohydrate, and 30 percent fat.

4. Amount of TAG at Each Meal and Snack

Read the table the way you read a mileage table found in maps. Match the desired calorie level in the left column with the percent equal to your meal and snack size listed at the top. Follow the example and you will be able to identify how much TAG you need.

Example	%	TAG	Your Meals	%	TAG
Breakfast	25%	70½	Breakfast	⎯⎯	⎯⎯
Snack			Snack	⎯⎯	⎯⎯
Lunch	30%	86	Lunch	⎯⎯	⎯⎯
Snack			Snack	⎯⎯	⎯⎯
Supper	35%	101	Supper	⎯⎯	⎯⎯
Snack	+ 10%	+ 30	Snack	+⎯⎯	+⎯⎯
Total	100%	287½ TAG	Total	100%	⎯⎯TAG

Most people find it very difficult to consume the high-carbohydrate, low-fat diet. This is not particularly surprising for the person who has diabetes. For years, people have been advised not to eat starchy foods. You may have been told to simply avoid carbohydrates. That's easy to say, but you have to get your calories from somewhere!

AMOUNT OF TAG FOR MEALS AND SNACKS
15% Protein, 55% Carbohydrate, 30% Fat

Calories	TAG	10%	15%	20%	25%	30%	35%
1000	166½	15	25	35	40½	50½	60½
1100	182	20	25	35	45½	55½	65½
1200	197	20	30	40½	50½	60½	70½
1300	207	20	30	40½	50½	65½	70½
1400	232½	25	35	45½	55½	70½	81
1500	247½	25	35	50½	60½	76	86
1600	257½	25	40	50½	65½	76	91
1700	278	30	40	55½	70½	86	96
1800	293	30	45½	60½	70½	86	101
1900	303	30	45½	60½	76	91	106
2000	323	30	50½	65½	81	96	111
2100	338½	35	50½	65½	86	101	116
2200	358½	35	55½	70½	91	106	126½

AMOUNT OF TAG FOR MEALS AND SNACKS
15% Protein, 55% Carbohydrate, 30% Fat

Calories	TAG	10%	15%	20%	25%	30%	35%
2300	373½	35	55½	76	91	111	131½
2400	389	40	60½	76	96	116	136½
2500	409	40	60½	81	101	121	141½
2600	424	40	65½	86	106	126½	146½
2700	439½	45	65½	86	111	131½	151½
2800	454½	45	70½	91	116	136½	157
2900	475	50	70½	96	121	141½	166½
3000	490	50	76	96	121	146½	171½
3100	510	50	76	101	126½	151½	176½
3200	525	55	81	106	131½	157	182

5. Milk Preferences

Milk is a very nutritious food. Ten TAG of milk may be just the food to have when you suspect that your blood sugar is low. One of the advantages of the TAG system is that you have the flexibility to include and exclude milk as you choose. Two servings each day are recommended. Lucy wants milk for breakfast and snack. When do you want milk?

Example	TAG	Milk?	Your Meals	TAG	Milk?
Breakfast	70½	yes	Breakfast	____	____
Snack			Snack	____	____
Lunch	86	no	Lunch	____	____
Snack			Snack	____	____
Supper	101	no	Supper	____	____
Snack	+ 30	yes	Snack	+ ____	____
Total	287½		Total	____	

6. Distribution of TAG Among Food Groups

Select the meat, milk, starch, sugar, and fat combination that matches the desired TAG. Matching the TAG leads to your meal plan. If you decide to change your calorie level, meal size, calorie distribution, or milk preference, you can follow the same steps to find the meal plan that best meets your needs.

Example	TAG	Meat	Milk	Starch	Sugar	Fat
Breakfast	70½	5	10	45	10	½
Lunch	86	10	0	60	15	1
Supper	101	10	0	70	20	1
Snack	+ 30	+ 0	+10	+ 15	+ 0	+0
Total	287½	25	20	190	45	2½

Your Meals	TAG	Meat	Milk	Starch	Sugar	Fat
Breakfast	——	——	——	——	——	——
Snack	——	——	——	——	——	——
Lunch	——	——	——	——	——	——
Snack	——	——	——	——	——	——
Supper	——	——	——	——	——	——
Snack	+——	+——	+——	+——	+——	+——
Total	——	——	——	——	——	——

At least twenty-five hundred meal plans can be derived from these tables. It is hoped that your increased input into the meal-plan design will help.

MEAL PATTERN WITH MILK
15% Protein, 55% Carbohydrate, 30% Fat

TAG	Meat	Milk	Starch	Sugar	Fat	Calories
30	5	5	20	0	0	185
35	5	5	20	5	0	215
40½	5	5	25	5	½	245
45½	5	5	30	5	½	280
50½	5	5	30	10	½	310
55½	5	5	35	10	½	340
60½	5	5	40	10	½	370
65½	5	10	40	10	½	400
70½	5	10	45	10	½	430
76	5	10	45	15	1	465
81	5	10	50	15	1	495
86	10	10	50	15	1	525
91	10	10	55	15	1	555
96	10	10	60	15	1	585
101	10	10	60	20	1	615
106	10	15	60	20	1	645
111	10	15	65	20	1	675
116	10	15	70	20	1	710
121	10	15	75	20	1	740
126½	10	15	75	25	1½	770
131½	10	15	80	25	1½	800
136½	10	15	85	25	1½	835
141½	15	15	85	25	1½	865
146½	15	15	90	25	1½	895
151½	15	20	90	25	1½	925
157	15	20	95	25	2	960
162	15	20	100	25	2	990
167	15	20	100	30	2	1020
172	15	20	105	30	2	1050
182	15	20	110	35	2	1110

MEAL PATTERN WITHOUT MILK
15% Protein, 55% Carbohydrate, 30% Fat

TAG	Meat	Starch	Sugar	Fat	Calories
30	5	20	0	0	185
35	5	25	5	0	215
40½	5	30	5	½	245
45½	5	30	10	½	280
50½	5	35	10	½	310
55½	10	35	10	½	340
60½	10	40	10	½	370
65½	10	45	10	½	400
70½	10	45	15	½	430
76	10	50	15	1	465
81	10	55	15	1	495
86	10	60	15	1	525
91	10	60	20	1	555
96	10	65	20	1	585
101	10	70	20	1	615
106	15	70	20	1	645
111	15	75	20	1	675
116	15	75	25	1	710
121	15	80	25	1	740
126½	15	85	25	1½	770
131½	15	90	25	1½	800
136½	15	95	25	1½	835
141½	15	95	30	1½	865
146½	15	100	30	1½	895
151½	20	100	30	1½	925
157	20	105	30	2	960
162	20	110	30	2	990
167	20	110	35	2	1020
172	20	115	35	2	1050
182	20	125	35	2	1110

SNACK PATTERNS

		with milk			without milk	
TAG	Calories	Meat	Milk	Starch	Meat	Starch
15	105	0	15	0	0	15
20	140	0	20	0	0	20
25	175	0	10	15	5	20
30	205	0	10	20	5	25
35	240	0	15	20	5	30
40	275	0	15	25	5	35
45	310	0	15	30	5	40
50	345	0	15	35	5	45
55	380	5	15	35	10	45

MEAL PLANS
15% Protein, 55% Carbohydrate, 30% Fat
25% Breakfast, 30% Lunch, 35% Supper, 10% Snack

1000 Calories = 166½ TAG

Meal	TAG	Meat	Milk	Starch	Sugar	Fat
Breakfast	40½	5	5	25	5	½
Lunch	50½	5	0	35	10	½
Supper	60½	10	0	40	10	½
Snack	+ 15	0	15	0	0	0
Total	166½					

1200 Calories = 201½ TAG

Meal	TAG	Meat	Milk	Starch	Sugar	Fat
Breakfast	50½	5	5	30	10	½
Lunch	60½	10	0	40	10	½
Supper	70½	10	0	45	15	½
Snack	+ 20	0	20	0	0	0
Total	201½					

1400 Calories = 232 TAG

Meal	TAG	Meat	Milk	Starch	Sugar	Fat
Breakfast	55½	5	5	35	10	½
Lunch	70½	10	0	45	15	½
Supper	81	10	0	55	15	1
Snack	+ 25	0	10	15	0	0
Total	232					

1600 Calories = 257½ TAG

Meal	TAG	Meat	Milk	Starch	Sugar	Fat
Breakfast	65½	5	10	40	10	½
Lunch	76	10	0	50	15	1
Supper	91	10	0	60	20	1
Snack	+ 25	0	10	15	0	0
Total	257½					

1800 Calories = 297½ TAG

Meal	TAG	Meat	Milk	Starch	Sugar	Fat
Breakfast	70½	5	10	45	10	½
Lunch	86	10	0	60	15	1
Supper	101	10	0	70	20	1
Snack	+ 30	0	10	20	0	0
Total	287½					

MEAL PLANS
15% Protein, 55% Carbohydrate, 30% Fat
25% Breakfast, 30% Lunch, 35% Supper, 10% Snack

2000 Calories = 318 TAG

Meal	TAG	Meat	Milk	Starch	Sugar	Fat
Breakfast	81	5	10	50	15	1
Lunch	96	10	0	65	20	1
Supper	111	15	0	75	20	1
Snack	+ 30	0	10	20	0	0
Total	318					

2200 Calories = 358½ TAG

Meal	TAG	Meat	Milk	Starch	Sugar	Fat
Breakfast	91	10	10	55	15	1
Lunch	106	15	0	70	20	1
Supper	126½	15	0	85	25	1½
Snack	+ 35	0	15	20	0	0
Total	358½					

2400 Calories = 388½ TAG

Meal	TAG	Meat	Milk	Starch	Sugar	Fat
Breakfast	96	10	10	60	15	1
Lunch	116	15	0	75	25	1
Supper	136½	15	0	95	25	1½
Snack	+ 40	0	15	25	0	0
Total	388½					

2600 Calories = 419 TAG

Meal	TAG	Meat	Milk	Starch	Sugar	Fat
Breakfast	106	10	15	60	20	1
Lunch	126½	15	0	85	25	1½
Supper	146½	15	0	100	30	1½
Snack	+ 40	0	15	25	0	0
Total	419					

2800 Calories = 454½ TAG

Meal	TAG	Meat	Milk	Starch	Sugar	Fat
Breakfast	116	10	15	70	20	1
Lunch	136½	15	0	95	25	1½
Supper	157	20	0	105	30	2
Snack	+ 45	0	15	30	0	0
Total	454½					

3000 Calories = 489½ TAG

Meal	TAG	Meat	Milk	Starch	Sugar	Fat
Breakfast	121	10	15	75	20	1
Lunch	146½	15	0	100	30	1½
Supper	172	20	0	115	35	2
Snack	+ 50	0	15	35	0	0
Total	489½					

MEAL PLANS
15% Protein, 55% Carbohydrate, 30% Fat
25% Breakfast, 30% Lunch, 35% Supper, 10% Snack

3200 Calories = 525½ TAG

Meal	TAG	Meat	Milk	Starch	Sugar	Fat
Breakfast	131½	10	15	80	25	1½
Lunch	157	20	0	105	30	2
Supper	182.0	20	0	125	35	2
Snack	+ 55	5	15	35	0	0
Total	525½					

It's Time to Eat!

Select the foods and use the meal plan that you have developed or simply follow the example of the 1800-calorie (20 percent protein, 45 percent carbohydrate, and 35 percent fat) meal plan.

1800 Calories = 260 TAG

Meal	TAG	Meat	Milk	Starch	Sugar	Fat
Breakfast	66½	10	10	35	10	1½
Lunch	76½	15	0	45	15	1½
Supper	92	15	0	55	20	2
Snack	+ 25	0	10	15	0	0
Total	260.0					

There are several different ways to determine food portions. Lucy will use a combination of the methods to illustrate all options. Through the examples you will be able to identify the most convenient method for you to count TAG and determine food portions. All information is derived from the food tables in the back of the book.

The distribution of TAG among the food groups of meat, milk, starch, sugar, and fat is somewhat flexible.

The only restrictions are:

1. TAG from the sugar group should not be greater than the specified amount.

2. TAG from the meat group should not be greater than the specified amount. Increase milk if you select a meal with a smaller amount of meat. Milk can be used at anytime to match any TAG goals.

3. TAG from the fat group should be omitted when the meat is high in fat. This is indicated in the food table by three stars (***) under fat. Fat may be omitted from one meal and used in another meal.

4. The total TAG should be within 5 percent of the meal TAG goal.

The goal is for the meal to provide a predictable amount of glucose. This is achieved by adding TAG until you reach the specified amount. You want the meals to be "well balanced." Lucy has selected All-Bran cereal, strawberries, almonds, and 2%-fat milk for breakfast. The following tables illustrate the information derived directly from the food tables. Use "TAG and Calorie Content of Common Portions" (page 137) to find the TAG value of average portions. Almonds are in the meat group. Milk is in the milk group. Cereal and fruit are in the starch group.

TAG and Calorie Content of Common Portions

Food	Measure	Grams	Ounces	TAG	Calories	Fat
All-Bran	½ cup	35	1.2	16.4	90	
strawberries	1 cup	149	5.2	10.3	45	
2%-fat milk	1 cup	244	8.6	16.9	122	*
almonds	12–15	25	0.5	5.3	90	***

Begin by adding common food portions.

Food	Measure		Weight		TAG
All-Bran	½ cup	=	35 grams	=	16.4 TAG
strawberries	1 cup	=	149 grams	=	10.3 TAG
2%-fat milk	1 cup	=	244 grams	=	16.9 TAG
almonds	12–15	=	15 grams	=	+ 5.3 TAG
			Subtotal	=	48.9 TAG

Lucy has a goal of 66½ TAG for breakfast. One possibility is to increase the All-Bran cereal to one cup. This increases the subtotal to 65.3 TAG.

Meal	TAG	Meat	Milk	Starch	Sugar	Fat
Breakfast	66½	10	10	35	10	1½

All-Bran	½ cup	=	35 grams	=	16.4 TAG
strawberries	1 cup	=	149 grams	=	10.3 TAG
2%-fat milk	1 cup	=	244 grams	=	16.9 TAG
almonds	12–15	=	15 grams	=	+ 5.3 TAG
			Subtotal	=	48.9 TAG
All-Bran	½ cup	=	35 grams	=	+16.4 TAG
			Total	=	65.3 TAG

Lucy can get the extra TAG by having an extra strawberry. Does the meal pass the restrictions?

1. Do not exceed sugar TAG.
   The meal did not contain any foods from the sugar group.

2. Do not exceed meat TAG.
   Almonds contained 5.3 TAG, which was less than the 10 TAG allowed. Milk was increased.

3. The fat group was omitted. Almonds are very high in fat as indicated by ***.

4. The meal TAG is within 5 percent of the goal.

What is your breakfast TAG requirement? If you had selected these foods, what portions would satisfy your goal?

Meal	TAG	Meat	Milk	Starch	Sugar	Fat
Breakfast	____	____	____	____	____	____

Food	Measure	Weight	TAG
All-Bran	____	____	____
strawberries	____	____	____
2%-fat milk	____	____	____
almonds	____	____	+ ____
		Total =	____ TAG

Does your meal pass the restrictions?

1. Do not exceed sugar TAG.

2. Do not exceed meat TAG.

3. The fat group can be omitted.

4. Meal TAG within 5 percent of goal.

A second method can be used to determine the food portions. Weigh the amount of food that you would like directly into the serving dish. Multiply the weight times TAG/gram or TAG/ounce to determine the TAG for the specific amount of food. Add TAG until you reach your goal. This has the advantage of being much more flexible to match individualized food portions. Find the factors to convert grams or ounces of food to TAG in the table "TAG Factors—Food Weights to TAG" (page 158). Once again, the foods are divided into the food groups of meat, milk, starch, sugar, and fat.

Food	TAG/gram	TAG/ounce
All-Bran	0.47	13.7
strawberries	0.07	2.0
2%-fat milk	0.07	2.0
almonds	0.35	10.6

Lucy has a scale that weighs in ounces. She begins by pouring the cereal into the bowl. The amount of TAG in the cereal is determined by multiplying the weight times TAG/ounce. The cereal weighs 2 ounces ($2 \times 13.7 = 27.4$ TAG). She adds the milk which weighs 6 ounces ($6 \times 2.0 = 12.0$ TAG). She adds the strawberries which weigh 5 ounces ($5 \times 2.0 = 10.0$ TAG). She adds the almonds which weigh 1 ounce (10.6 TAG).

Food	Weight		TAG/ounce	=	TAG
All-Bran	2 ounces	×	13.7	=	27.4
2%-fat milk	6 ounces	×	2.0	=	12.0
strawberries	5 ounces	×	2.0	=	10.0
almonds	1 ounce	×	10.6	=	+10.6
			Subtotal	=	60.0 TAG

Lucy can consult the same food table to find food portions equal to a specific amount of TAG. She needs 6 TAG to reach her goal. The table is set up like a mileage table. Rather than relating two cities and finding the distance in miles, you match the food listed on the left with a specific amount of TAG listed at the top to find the grams of food equal to the specific amount of TAG.

Grams of Food Equal to TAG

Food	5	10	15	20	25	30
All-Bran	7	13	20	26	33	39
strawberries	67	134	202	269	336	403
2%-fat milk	72	145	217	289	362	434
almonds	14	28	42	56	70	84

Milk is an excellent food for Lucy to use to reach her goal. It is easy to portion. What portion of milk equals 6 TAG?

$$
\begin{array}{lllll}
5 \text{ TAG} & & & = & 72 \text{ grams} \\
+ \underline{1 \text{ TAG}} & = & 10\% \text{ of } 145 \text{ grams} & = & +\underline{15 \text{ grams}} \\
6 \text{ TAG} & & & = & 87 \text{ grams}
\end{array}
$$

Lucy's scale weighs in ounces: 1 ounce equals 28.45 grams. Lucy needs an additional 3 ounces of milk to reach her TAG goal (87 grams of milk ÷ 28.45 grams per ounce = 3.06 ounces of milk). The math of dividing 87 by 28.45 is much more complicated that it needs to be. Simplify the math by rounding off numbers. Round off 87 grams of milk to 90 grams of milk. Round off 28.45 grams per ounce to 30 grams per ounce (90 grams of milk ÷ 30 grams = 3 ounces of milk). The math is much, much easier without compromising the accuracy.

Food decisions can be based on the quantity of food that you want to eat. Consider how the following juices relate to each other. If you needed 10 TAG, you could drink 65 grams (2 ounces) of grape juice or 218 grams (7 ounces) of tomato juice.

Grams of Food Equal to TAG

Food	5	10	15	20	25	30
apple juice	43	85	128	170	213	255
grape juice	33	65	98	131	163	196
grapefruit juice	52	104	156	208	260	312
orange juice	49	98	147	196	245	294
tomato juice	109	218	328	437	546	655

Juices are ideal to satisfy a precise TAG requirement. Beverages are so easy to portion. You can use this table to determine a portion equal to any amount of TAG through simple math of TAG. If you want to weigh in ounces, one ounce equals about 30 grams.

What portion of apple juice contains 20 TAG?
What portion of grape juice contains 22 TAG?
What portion of grapefruit juice contains 11 TAG?
What portion of tomato juice contains 8 TAG?

Answers:

170 grams of apple juice contain 20 TAG

144 grams of grape juice contain 22 TAG

	20 TAG			=		131 grams
+	2 TAG	=	10% of 131 grams	=	+	13 grams
	22 TAG			=		144 grams

114 grams of grapefruit juice contain 11 TAG

	10 TAG			=		104 grams
+	1 TAG	=	10% of 104 grams	=	+	10 grams
	11 TAG			=		114 grams

174 grams of tomato juice contain 8 TAG

	10 TAG			=		218 grams
−	2 TAG	=	10% of 437 grams	=	−	44 grams
	8 TAG			=		174 grams

Lucy wants to pack her lunch. She has selected a sandwich with bologna, cheese, whole-wheat bread, and mayonnaise, a banana, and graham crackers. The following table is derived from "TAG and Calorie Content of Common Portions" (page 137). Whole-wheat bread, graham crackers, and the banana are

in the starch group. Bologna and cheese are in the meat group.
Mayonnaise is in the fat group.

TAG and Calorie Content of Common Portions

Food	Measure	Grams	Oz.	TAG	Calories	Fat
whole-wheat bread	1 slice	23	0.8	12.5	56	
bologna	1 slice	28	1.0	3.1	88	***
cheese, "lite"	1 slice	28	1.0	5.9	70	**
mayonnaise	1 tbl.	14	0.5	1.5	101	***
banana	1 medium	114	4.0	27.5	105	
graham crackers	2 squares	14	0.5	11.1	54	*

Begin by adding common portions. Simplify the math by rounding off numbers. Do not round off the TAG from the fat group. Fat is high in calories and low in TAG. One half TAG of fat equals 45 calories!

whole-wheat bread	2 slices	=	46 grams	=	25 TAG
bologna	1 slice	=	28 grams	=	3 TAG
cheese, "lite"	1 slice	=	28 grams	=	6 TAG
mayonnaise	1 tbl.	=	14 grams	=	1½ TAG
banana	1 medium	=	114 grams	=	28 TAG
graham crackers	2 squares	=	14 grams	=	+11 TAG
			Subtotal	=	74½ TAG

Compare the calculated TAG from each food group to the meal plan.

Meal	TAG	Meat	Milk	Starch	Sugar	Fat
lunch	76½	15	0	45	15	1½
Subtotal	74½	9	0	64	0	1½

Lucy could add another slice of bologna to match her TAG.

Total   77½   12   0   64   0   1½

Does the meal pass the restrictions?

1. Do not exceed sugar TAG.

2. Do not exceed meat TAG.

3. Omit TAG from fat when high fat meats are used. "Lite" cheese supplied half of the meat TAG. Fat does not have to be omitted. Also, breakfast was very low in fat.

4. Total meal TAG within 5 percent of goal.

Meal	TAG	Meat	Milk	Starch	Sugar	Fat
Your Lunch	——	——	——	——	——	——

Food	Measure	Weight	TAG
whole-wheat bread	——	——	——
mayonnaise	——	——	——
bologna	——	——	——
cheese, "lite"	——	——	——
banana	——	——	——
graham crackers	——	——	+ ——
		Total	= —— TAG

Have you ever thought that all bananas weigh exactly the same? You can easily determine exactly how much TAG is in a banana without having to peel it! If it is in the early morning and you are packing lunch, you certainly don't want to peel and weigh the banana. Who wants a mushy brown fruit for lunch! Use the TAG factor that has been adjusted to account for the peel. Multiply the weight in grams times the conversion factor of 0.15 TAG per gram. I just happen to have a bunch of bananas in the kitchen; they vary from 27 to 37 TAG!

Food		Weight		TAG/gram		TAG		Rounded off
banana #1	=	196 grams	×	0.15	=	29.4	=	29 TAG
banana #2	=	246 grams	×	0.15	=	36.9	=	37 TAG
banana #3	=	178 grams	×	0.15	=	26.7	=	27 TAG
banana #4	=	210 grams	×	0.15	=	31.5	=	32 TAG

The whole-wheat bread, cheese, bologna, mayonnaise, and graham crackers have a TAG value of 45.7. If Lucy had selected banana #2 of 37 TAG, the lunch would equal 82.7 TAG. Lucy's meal TAG is about six TAG greater than her goal of 76.5 TAG. If she deletes one graham cracker (5.5 TAG), she will reach her goal.

meal without the banana	=	45.7 TAG
banana #2	=	+37.0 TAG
Total	=	82.7 TAG
Meal Goal	=	−76.5 TAG
		6.2 TAG too high

Meal Plan, Lunch

Meal	TAG	Meat	Milk	Starch	Sugar	Fat
Lunch	76½	15	0	45	15	1½

Food		Weight		TAG
2 slices of whole-wheat bread	=	46 grams	=	25.0 TAG
1 square graham cracker	=	7 grams	=	6.0 TAG

Food		Weight		TAG
banana #2	=	246 grams	=	37.0 TAG
1 ounce bologna	=	28 grams	=	3.0 TAG
1 ounce cheese, "lite"	=	28 grams	=	6.0 TAG
½ tablespoon mayonnaise	=	7 grams	=	+ 0.7 TAG
				77.7 TAG

If Lucy had selected banana #3 containing 27 TAG, food would need to be added to the basic meal.

meal without the banana	=	45.7 TAG
banana #3	=	+27.0 TAG
Total	=	72.7 TAG

Meal Goal	=	76.5 TAG
Subtotal	=	−72.7 TAG
		3.8 TAG = 4 TAG too low

A couple of slices of tomato could be added: 74 grams of tomato contain 4 TAG.

Meal Plan, Lunch

Meal	TAG	Meat	Milk	Starch	Sugar	Fat
Lunch	76½	15	0	45	15	1½

Food		Weight		TAG
2 slices of whole-wheat bread	=	46 grams	=	25.0 TAG
2 squares graham crackers	=	7 grams	=	11.0 TAG
banana #3	=	178 grams	=	27.0 TAG
1 ounce bologna	=	28 grams	=	3.0 TAG
1 ounce cheese, lite	=	28 grams	=	6.0 TAG
½ tablespoon mayonnaise	=	7 grams	=	0.7 TAG
tomato slices	=	74 grams	=	+ 4.0 TAG
				76.7 TAG

When you first return from the grocery store, weigh and label the fruit with the TAG values. It will be easier when you pack your lunch. Also, it helps to see the relationship between food and TAG. Set priorities in weighing foods. Be most accurate with high TAG foods.

Conversion Factors for Fruit with Skins and Cores

Food	TAG/gram	TAG/ounce
apple with core	0.11	3.2
banana with peel	0.15	4.3
cherries with stones	0.13	3.7
dates with pit	0.65	18.2
grapefruit with skin	0.05	1.5
orange, navel with skin	0.09	2.6
orange, valencia with skin	0.14	4.1
peaches with pit	0.10	2.7
tangerine with skin	0.09	2.6

How much TAG is in each portion?

Food	Weight		TAG/gram		TAG
apple with core	200 grams	×	_____	=	____
banana with peel	180 grams	×	_____	=	____
orange, navel	200 grams	×	_____	=	____
tangerine	120 grams	×	_____	=	____

Answers:
Apple (22 TAG); banana (27 TAG); orange (18 TAG); tangerine (13.5 TAG).

What do you want to eat for supper? As a nutritionist, I spend a lot of time thinking about food. I am delighted that Jackson, my husband, prepares dinner during the week. He has the right idea. Make it simple and make it fast. "If it takes more than twenty minutes to prepare supper, eat supper, and do the dishes, it is too long!'' Jackson does this by preparing a few simple foods. Supper might be chicken, mixed vegetables, potatoes, and chocolate candy. Chicken is in the meat group. The potatoes and mixed vegetables are in the starch group. The chocolate candy is in the sugar group. Margarine could be added to the vegetables. Information on the individual foods comes from the food tables.

TAG and Calorie Content of Common Portions

Food	Measure	Grams	Ounce	TAG	Calories	Fat
chicken, light	3.5 oz.	100	3.5	18.4	173	*
mixed vegetables	⅔ cup	100	3.5	12.8	60	
potato, frozen	¾ cup	85	3.0	21.9	138	*
chocolate candy	1 ounce	28	1.0	18.7	160	**

TAG Factors—Food Weights to TAG

Food	TAG/gram	TAG/ounce						
			5	10	15	20	25	30
chicken, light	0.18	5.3	27	54	82	109	136	163
mixed vegetables	0.13	3.7	39	78	117	156	195	234
potato, frozen	0.26	7.3	19	39	58	78	97	117
chocolate candy	0.65	18.7	8	15	23	31	39	46

Grams of Food Equal to TAG

If Lucy came for supper, she would need 92 TAG.

Meal Plan, Supper

Meal	TAG	Meat	Milk	Starch	Sugar	Fat
Supper	92	15	0	55	20	2.0

Consider the meal restrictions.

1. TAG from the sugar group should not be greater than the specified amount. No more than 20 TAG can come from the sugar group.

2. TAG from the meat group should not be greater than the specified amount. No more than 15 TAG can come from the meat group.

3. TAG from the fat group should be omitted when the meat is high in fat. Chicken is low in fat as shown by one star (*). Up to 20 grams (⅔ ounce) of margarine can be used to prepare the chicken and serve at the meal.

4. The total TAG should be within 5 percent of the meal TAG goal.

Using the numbers from "Grams of Food Equal to TAG," Lucy finds that 82 grams (about 3 ounces) of chicken equals 15 TAG. Also, Lucy finds that 31 grams of chocolate candy equals 20 TAG.

Lucy considers the mixed vegetables and potatoes to be "average portions" and uses "TAG and Calorie Content of Common Portions" to determine the TAG value of those items. She has rounded off the TAG values of common portions to simplify the math. Adding the TAG values from each food, she discovers that she needs to add 22 TAG.

Food	Weight		TAG
chicken	82 grams	=	15 TAG
chocolate candy	31 grams	=	20 TAG
mixed vegetables	100 grams	=	13 TAG
potato, frozen shoestring	85 grams	= +	22 TAG
	Subtotal	=	70 TAG

Meal TAG	92 TAG
− Subtotal	− 70 TAG
Needed TAG	22 TAG

Making up the needed TAG can be done by increasing the portions of mixed vegetables and potatoes or by adding a food. One dinner roll has 17 TAG. Also, 2 TAG of margarine is added to bring the total to 89 TAG. This is within 5 percent of the goal of 92 TAG. If she wants, she can have a few more vegetables.

Food	Weight		TAG
chicken	82 grams	=	15 TAG
chocolate candy	31 grams	=	20 TAG
mixed vegetables	100 grams	=	13 TAG
potato, frozen shoestring	85 grams	= +	22 TAG
	Subtotal	=	70 TAG
margarine	20 grams	=	2 TAG
dinner roll	28 grams	= +	17 TAG
	Total	=	89 TAG

Snacks reduce elevations in blood glucose by reducing the amount of food consumed at one time. Blood glucose is much greater after a single 1800-calorie meal than the three meals and one snack divided as 450 calories, 540 calories, 630 calories, and 180 calories. Dairy products are excellent for snacks. The carbohydrate in milk will lead to a gentle increase in blood glucose, while the protein will keep the blood glucose from dropping rapidly.

Grams of Food Equal to Specific TAG

Food	5	10	15	20	25	30
plain yogurt	49	98	147	195	244	293
blueberries	34	69	103	137	171	206

The 25 TAG snack could be 98 grams of plain yogurt (10 TAG) with 103 grams of blueberries (15 TAG).

1800 Calories = 260 TAG

Meal	TAG	Meat	Milk	Starch	Sugar	Fat
breakfast	66½	10	10	35	10	1½
lunch	76½	15	0	45	15	1½
supper	92	15	0	55	20	2
snack	+ 25	0	10	15	0	0
Total	260					

Breakfast

Food	Weight		TAG
All Bran	70 grams	=	33 TAG
strawberries	149 grams	=	10 TAG
2%-fat milk	244 grams	=	17 TAG
almonds	15 grams	= +	5 TAG
	Total	=	65 TAG

Lunch

Food	Weight		TAG
whole-wheat bread	46 grams	=	25 TAG
graham crackers	7 grams	=	6 TAG
banana #2	246 grams	=	37 TAG
bologna	28 grams	=	3 TAG
cheese, "lite"	28 grams	=	6 TAG
mayonnaise	7 grams	= +	1 TAG
	Total	=	78 TAG

Supper

Food	Weight		TAG
chicken	82 grams	=	15 TAG
chocolate candy	31 grams	=	20 TAG
mixed vegetables	100 grams	=	13 TAG
potato, frozen shoestring	85 grams	=	22 TAG
margarine	20 grams	=	2 TAG
dinner roll	28 grams	= +	17 TAG
	Total	=	89 TAG

Snack

Food	Weight		TAG
plain yogurt	98 grams	=	10 TAG
blueberries	103 grams	= +	15 TAG
	Total	=	25 TAG

Numbers have been rounded off to the nearest whole number.

The Glucose-to-Insulin Ratio

Glucose is the food that your body uses for energy. All cells need glucose for energy. Insulin is the hormone that carries glucose from the bloodstream into the cells of the body. If your pancreas produces less insulin, the blood glucose will go up while the cells are left to starve.

To understand what insulin does, consider what happens when you don't have insulin around. First, the blood glucose goes up because glucose can't get into the cells to be used for energy. Blood glucose may go from a normal level of 90 mg/100 ml to as high as 300 to 1200 mg/100 ml.

Second, fats from fatty tissues move into the blood stream where they can be deposited into the walls of the blood vessels (atherosclerosis). People with diabetes have a much higher chance than the general population of getting atherosclerosis. This is why a low-fat diet is recommended even though we know that less insulin is required to use the calories from fat.

Third, less protein is deposited into muscle tissues. Without insulin, fats, glucose, and protein go into the blood stream while neglecting the nutrient needs of the individual cells. It is important for you to be able to relate insulin replacement to the dietary constituents of protein, carbohydrate, and fat. Total Available Glucose makes it possible for you to relate what you eat directly to your individual insulin requirement.

Having a daily routine is important in balancing insulin, food, and exercise for health. In the real world, our lives are always changing. Total Available Glucose will help you adjust insulin, food, and exercise to suit your changing needs.

By now you can design a basic meal plan that suits your schedule needs. Foods can be varied from the basic meal plan to suit your needs. As your life changes, you can make adjustments in insulin and exercise to achieve a normal blood glucose. Informed changes become smart decisions as you learn how to balance the variables.

Your insulin and TAG requirements are unique. They may change over time. For an estimate, use the following table relating insulin needs at the top to dietary TAG on the left-hand side as a starting point for determining the relationship between TAG and insulin.

GLUCOSE-TO-INSULIN RATIO
Insulin Requirement

Diet TAG	10	20	30	40	50	60	70	80	90	100
100	10	5	3	3	2	2	1	1	1	1
110	11	6	4	3	2	2	2	1	1	1
120	12	6	4	3	2	2	2	2	1	1
130	13	7	4	3	3	2	2	2	1	1
140	14	7	5	4	3	2	2	2	2	1
150	15	8	5	4	3	3	2	2	2	2
160	16	8	5	4	3	3	2	2	2	2
170	17	9	6	4	3	3	2	2	2	2
180	18	9	6	5	4	3	3	2	2	2
190	19	10	6	5	4	3	3	2	2	2
200	20	10	7	5	4	3	3	3	2	2
220	22	11	7	6	4	4	3	3	2	2
240	24	12	8	6	5	4	3	3	3	2
260	26	13	9	7	5	4	4	3	3	3
280	28	14	9	7	6	5	4	4	3	3

GLUCOSE-TO-INSULIN RATIO
Insulin Requirement

Diet TAG	10	20	30	40	50	60	70	80	90	100
300	30	15	10	8	6	5	4	4	3	3
320	32	16	11	8	6	5	5	4	4	3
340	34	17	11	9	7	6	5	4	4	3

Numbers have been rounded off to the nearest whole number.

For greater precision, use the following formula. Also, consult your doctor to help determine your glucose-to-insulin ratio.

G–I ratio = dietary TAG ÷ insulin requirement

Our example, Lucy, has a dietary intake of 264 TAG (1800 calories) each day. Her insulin requirement is 40 units each day. If she is not spilling any glucose in her urine, 40 units of insulin are required for her to use 264 TAG per day. Simply divide the TAG by the insulin to determine the glucose insulin ratio. Lucy has a G–I ratio of 6.6. One unit of insulin will cover 6.6 TAG.

264 TAG ÷ 40 Units = G–I ratio of 6.6

This is useful information to know. The holidays are around the corner. Lucy knows that she will be eating an extra 20 TAG. If her G–I ratio is 6.6, she will require an extra 3 units of insulin.

20 TAG ÷ 6.6 G–I ratio = 3 units of insulin

The Christmas holidays are over and Lucy has gained some weight. She wants to reduce her weight safely. If she reduces her food intake by 64 TAG per day, she will need to reduce her insulin by 10 units.

64 TAG ÷ 6.6 G–I ratio = 10 units of insulin

What is your G–I ratio?

dietary TAG_____ ÷ insulin_____ = _____ G–I ratio

If you were going to eat an extra 20 TAG, how much would you need to increase your insulin?

20 TAG ÷ _____ G–I ratio = _____ units of insulin

If you were going to reduce your dietary TAG by 64, how much would you need to decrease your insulin?

64 TAG ÷ _____ G–I ratio = _____ units of insulin

The purpose of any food pattern is to provide nutrition for optimal health. Food selection is a complex process and challenging task. The ideal food pattern can be sensitive to individual nutritional and lifestyle needs. This should include a large variety of foods from all food groups. It should be a system that helps you to achieve body weight for optimal health.

If you are spilling glucose in your urine, the G–I ratio will need to be slightly adjusted. If our example has a urine volume of 2000 ml per day and is spilling glucose at 1 percent, the amount of glucose spilled will equal 20 grams.

urine volume (2000) × percent (.01) = 20 grams

The actual number of TAG units utilized would be dietary intake minus the grams of glucose spilled.

Dietary Intake (264) − spilled (20) = 244 TAG Used

Keeping insulin constant at 40 units, the G–I ratio would equal TAG utilized divided by insulin = 6.1.

244 TAG used ÷ 40 units of insulin = 6.1 G–I ratio

The G–I ratio changed from 6.6 to 6.1. The G–I ratio changed by about 10 percent. As blood glucose is normalized, the G–I ratio will also decrease.

There are many factors that influence your blood glucose. Consult your doctor to help determine your G–I ratio.

Walk Up the Steps? You Have Got to Be Kidding!

Exercise is fundamental to good health. Exercise keeps you strong. Exercise lowers blood glucose by a combination of burning calories and increasing the transport of glucose into the muscle cells. Consult your doctor when you begin an exercise program. Adjustments in diet and/or insulin may need to be made.

Special equipment or scheduling of your time is not essential. It is easy to make exercise a part of your day. The opportunities are everywhere!

Increase exercise by walking up the stairs. It may sound trite, but it truly is just a series of steps. You may be thinking, "Where are the stairs?" All buildings with multiple floors have them for safety reasons. Know where the stairs are located in the unlikely but possible event of a fire. For safety—take the time to find the stairs.

"The elevator is here! It's easier!" It is rare for the elevator door to be open the moment you appear. Taking the elevator often means standing and waiting. "I have walked half a flight of stairs. My heart is pounding." The first time up the stairs will be hardest. Use good judgment. Fitness improves quickly but it does take some time. In time, you will be amused to discover that locating the stairs may have been the hardest part!

Your destination is the sixth floor. You have not exercised in a long time. Don't charge up six flights and be exhausted at the top. Climb one flight. Rest. Climb the second flight. Take the elevator the rest of the way. As you become fit, the distance will become much easier. Recognize stair climbing as an opportunity to include exercise sensibly into your day. It becomes easier as you increase your strength, decrease your weight, and increase your confidence. Go down the stairs too. It's very easy.

Driving has replaced much walking. The automobile has greatly increased our mobility. By car, we see and do much more than if we were limited to walking. Do this simple thing to increase exercise: Park the car on the opposite side of the parking lot. There is little competition for that space. The time to walk the extra steps is very little. Make exercise a part of your day.

Where do you live, work, play, and shop? Are there times when you could walk to the corner store? Looking for a place to park may take more time than the walk. Of course, there are times when walking is not practical. I live six miles from work and it is not realistic to walk there. However, I can park the car a half mile away from work. Walking is easy when it is a habit. Use a stopwatch for a few days to discover how much time you spend walking. And use your imagination!

We have so many step savers that we may find ourselves driving to a gym to put the steps back in. Ironic. But of the many forms of exercise available, gym classes can be most enjoyable for the comradeship. I primarily encourage you to identify the step savers in your day that can be replaced by exercise. Make it a habit today.

TAG and calories are simply two ways of measuring the amount of energy that comes from food. Exercise requires energy. The intensity of the exercise changes the amount of TAG or calories burned: Walking quickly burns more calories or

TAG than walking slowly. Energy burned also varies when you play tennis: A game of singles would probably be more strenuous than a doubles game. Certainly, energy burned varies with the golfer who drives a cart and the golfer who walks and carries a bag.

Your body weight also changes the amount of energy burned. It requires more energy to carry a body that weighs two hundred forty pounds up ten flights of steps than to carry a body that weighs one hundred twenty pounds.

You may be familiar with tables that tell you how many calories are burned doing specific activities for a specific amount of time. The following table shows the number of calories that are burned if you walk a mile at a specific rate. This is also adjusted to your individual weight.

CALORIES BURNED PER MILE OF WALKING

Rate	100 pounds	120 pounds	140 pounds	160 pounds	200 pounds
2.0 mph	43	51	55	60	68
2.5 mph	45	52	57	62	72
3.0 mph	47	54	59	64	76
3.5 mph	49	56	61	65	78
4.0 mph	51	57	62	69	82

For example, if Lucy weighs one hundred twenty pounds and walks a mile at the rate of three miles per hour, she will burn 54 calories. Calories can be directly related to TAG. Consider the diet that has a calorie distribution of 20 percent protein, 45 percent carbohydrate, and 35 percent fat. There are 145 TAG for every 1000 calories. Convert calories to TAG by dividing by 6.9.

1 TAG = 1000 calories ÷ 145 TAG = 6.9 calories

Lucy would burn 7.8 TAG if she walked one mile at the rate of three miles per hour.

$$51 \text{ calories} \div 6.9 = 7.8 \text{ TAG}$$

The table showing the amount of calories burned per mile of walking is converted to TAG in the same manner. Divide each calorie level by 6.9.

TAG BURNED PER MILE OF WALKING

Rate	100 pounds	120 pounds	140 pounds	160 pounds	200 pounds
2.0 mph	6.2	7.4	8.0	8.7	10.0
2.5 mph	6.5	7.5	8.3	9.0	10.4
3.0 mph	6.8	7.8	8.6	9.3	11.0
3.5 mph	7.1	8.1	8.8	9.4	11.3
4.0 mph	7.4	8.3	9.0	10.0	11.9

Writing about exercise has just inspired me to get up from sitting at the computer to go for a bicycle ride. It certainly brings home the point of some of the variables to be discovered when trying to estimate TAG burned per activity. One bike has balloon tires while the other has skinny tires. I chose the skinny tires but spent a few minutes pumping them up. Charleston is in the "low country." The bridges are the hills. It was pretty windy. More TAG was burned going against the wind versus having the wind behind me. The traffic wasn't bad so I didn't spend much time at stoplights. I enjoy riding a bike because the distance traveled keeps one from getting bored and the wind is cooling as you go.

Sitting at a computer may have frustrations but it does not burn up many calories. Can you tell the difference between being mentally tired and physically tired? Take a critical look at how you spend time. Negotiate with yourself to identify acceptable modifications that improve health.

Select the activity that suits you. If you do not enjoy the activity, you will probably not do it. Get moving and enjoy!

The following table indicates the amount of TAG burned per minute of activity. Also, the number of minutes of the activity required to burn the specific amounts of 10, 20, 30, and 40 TAG are shown. The numbers were derived assuming that 6.9 calories are equal to one TAG. The numbers are averages. It is most helpful as a means of comparing activities. The table reads like a mileage table of a road map. Match the activity listed on the left with the TAG listed at the top to find the minutes of activity equal to the specific TAG.

MINUTES OF ACTIVITY EQUAL TO SPECIFIC TAG

Activity	TAG/Minute	10 TAG	20 TAG	30 TAG	40 TAG
Walking 3.0 mph	0.4	26	51	77	103

You burn 0.4 TAG for every minute that you walk at the rate of three miles per hour. You need to walk for twenty-six minutes at this rate to burn 10 TAG.

MINUTES OF ACTIVITY EQUAL TO SPECIFIC TAG

Activity	TAG/ Minute	10 TAG	20 TAG	30 TAG	40 TAG
Archery	0.5	20	41	61	82
Backpacking	1.3	8	16	23	31
Badminton	1.0	10	20	30	40
Basketball	1.2	9	17	26	34
Bicycling	0.9	11	23	34	46
Bowling	0.4	26	51	77	103
Calisthenics	0.9	11	23	34	46
Canoeing	0.9	11	23	34	46
Dancing	0.7	14	27	41	54
Fishing, boat	0.4	26	51	77	103
Fishing, stream	0.8	12	24	36	48
Football, touch	1.3	8	16	23	31
Golf, power cart	0.3	33	67	100	133
Golf, walking	0.8	12	24	36	48

MINUTES OF ACTIVITY EQUAL TO SPECIFIC TAG

Activity	TAG/ Minute	10 TAG	20 TAG	30 TAG	40 TAG
Handball	1.7	6	12	18	24
Hiking	0.7	14	27	41	54
Horseback riding	0.9	11	23	34	46
Mountain climbing	1.2	9	17	26	34
Ping-Pong	0.6	18	36	55	73
Racquetball	1.7	6	12	18	24
Running					
5.0-minute mile	3.4	3	6	9	12
5.5-minute mile	3.0	3	7	10	13
6.0-minute mile	2.7	4	7	11	15
7.5-minute mile	2.1	5	9	14	19
8.5-minute mile	1.9	5	11	16	21
10.0-minute mile	1.6	6	13	19	25
11.0-minute mile	1.3	8	15	23	30
Running					
12.0 mph	3.4	3	6	9	12
10.9 mph	3.0	3	7	10	13
10.0 mph	2.7	4	7	11	15
8.0 mph	2.1	5	9	14	19
7.0 mph	1.9	5	11	16	21
6.0 mph	1.6	6	13	19	25
5.5 mph	1.3	8	15	23	30
Sailing	0.5	22	43	65	87
Scuba diving	1.2	9	17	26	34
Shuffleboard	0.3	33	67	100	133
Skating, roller	1.2	9	17	26	34

MINUTES OF ACTIVITY EQUAL TO SPECIFIC TAG

Activity	TAG/ Minute	10 TAG	20 TAG	30 TAG	40 TAG
Skiing					
cross-country	1.5	7	14	20	27
downhill	1.2	9	17	26	34
Soccer	1.3	8	15	23	31
Softball	0.7	15	30	45	60
Squash	1.7	6	12	18	24
Stair-climbing	0.9	11	21	32	43
Swimming	0.9	11	21	32	43
Tennis	1.0	10	20	30	40
Volleyball	0.7	15	30	45	60
Walking					
30-minute mile	0.2	45	91	136	182
24-minute mile	0.3	34	69	103	138
20-minute mile	0.4	26	51	77	103
17-minute mile	0.5	22	43	65	87
15-minute mile	0.7	15	31	46	62
12-minute mile	1.1	9	19	28	38
Walking					
2.0 mph	0.2	45	91	136	182
2.5 mph	0.3	34	69	103	138
3.0 mph	0.4	26	51	77	103
3.5 mph	0.5	22	43	65	87
4.0 mph	0.7	15	31	46	62
5.0 mph	1.1	9	19	28	38

The Switch: Exchanges to TAG

Food Exchange Lists, known as the ADA Exchange System, were developed in 1950 by the joint efforts of the American Diabetes Association, the American Dietetic Association, and the Diabetes Section of the U.S. Public Health Service. The lists were designed to simplify food selection while increasing flexibility and improving standardization. The food tables were revised in 1986. As with TAG, the meal plan is based on your individual calorie requirement and meal pattern.

There are six food groups in the Food Exchange Lists system. Also, the meat group and milk group are further divided into three subgroups each.

Exchange	Portion
meat (lean, medium-fat, high-fat)	1 ounce
milk (skim, low-fat, whole)	1 cup
starch/bread	1 slice
fruit	1 medium
vegetable	1 cup
fat	1 pat

Meals and snacks throughout the day are based on combinations of exchanges. The number of food exchanges varies to match individual calorie levels. The number of food groups are arranged to assure an appropriate calorie distribution.

Each food exchange is assigned a protein, carbohydrate, and fat value based on the average nutrient content. You can convert your dietary pattern into TAG by adding the TAG content of each food group. The TAG values of each food exchange are based on the sum of 58 percent of the grams of protein, 100 percent of the grams of carbohydrate, and 10 percent of the grams of fat. Calories are equal to the sum of grams of protein times four, grams of carbohydrate times four, and grams of fat times nine.

Food Group	Protein	Carbo-hydrate	Fat	TAG	Calories
Meat, lean meat,	7 grams	0 grams	3 grams	4.4	55
medium-fat	7 grams	0 grams	5 grams	4.6	75
meat, high-fat	7 grams	0 grams	7 grams	4.9	100
milk, skim	8 grams	12 grams	0 grams	16.6	80
milk, low-fat	8 grams	12 grams	5 grams	17.1	125
milk, whole	8 grams	12 grams	8 grams	17.4	150
starch/bread	3 grams	15 grams	0 grams	16.8	70
fruit	0 grams	15 grams	0 grams	15.0	45
vegetable	2 grams	5 grams	0 grams	6.2	30
fat	0 grams	0 grams	5 grams	0.5	45

Using the ADA Exchange System, a meal might be three breads, one fruit, two vegetables, four lean meats, and one fat.

Meal	# Exchange	TAG		TAG/meal	Percent
meat, lean	4	× 4.4	=	17.6	18%
starch/bread	3	× 16.8	=	50.4	53%
fruit	1	× 15.0	=	15.0	16%
vegetable	2	× 6.2	=	12.4	13%
fat	1	× 0.5	=	+ 0.5	<1%
		Total	=	95.9 TAG	

Even if you do not switch to TAG, you will find it helpful to know the TAG value of each exchange. It will give you a clear way to relate individual foods to the impact on blood glucose. In this particular example, the three starch/bread exchanges equals 50 TAG or a little more than half of the TAG for the meal.

The estimated calorie content of the meal is 570 calories.

Meal	# Exchange		Calories		Cal/ meal	Per-cent
meat, lean	4	×	55	=	220	39%
starch/ bread	3	×	70	=	210	37%
fruit	1	×	45	=	45	8%
vegetable	2	×	25	=	50	9%
fat	1	×	45	= +	45	8%
			Total	=	570 Calories	

Meat and fat combined equal 47 percent of calories while only 19 percent of TAG! This illustrates that matching TAG will control blood glucose but that the dietary system is also based on an appropriate distribution of calorie source. Fat leads to a small amount of TAG but is very high in calories! Extra calories lead to weight gain.

A typical 1400-calorie diet might include five breads, four vegetables, three fruits, six meats, two milks, and three fats.

Day	# Exchange		Calories		Cal/ day	Per-cent
meat, medium-fat	6	×	75	=	450	32%
milk, low-fat	2	×	125	=	250	18%
starch/ bread	5	×	70	=	350	25%
fruit	3	×	45	=	135	10%
vegetable	4	×	25	=	100	7%
fat	3	×	45	= +	135	10%
			Total	=	1420 Calories	

This 1400-calorie diet contains 216 TAG.

Day	# Exchange	TAG		TAG/day	Percent
meat, medium-fat	6	× 4.6	=	27.6	13%
milk, low-fat	2	× 17.1	=	34.2	16%
starch/bread	5	× 16.8	=	84.0	39%
fruit	3	× 15.0	=	45.0	21%
vegetable	4	× 6.2	=	24.8	11%
fat	3	× 0.5	=	+ 1.5	1%
		Total	=	217.1 TAG	

If you are currently on the ADA Exchange System, you can switch to TAG by matching the TAG content of your current diet. Certainly, consult your doctor, dietitian, and/or nurse-educator when making changes in your diet. They will be pleased to provide guidance and support as you actively make smart food decisions!

With the ADA Exchange System you count six different food groups with additional subgroups. The starch/bread, fruit, and vegetable groups have been combined with TAG. This greatly increases flexibility without compromising accuracy. Variety is always encouraged.

It is usual for a person who has just been diagnosed with diabetes to be compulsive about the many changes required to balance diet and insulin to keep blood sugars normal. It is an unjustified frustration for people to have to spend time wondering how to eat more strawberries because they are in season! Select the foods and portions that you want. Match your planned TAG. Limit fats. The food system will provide you with improved accuracy while increasing flexibility.

We consume a great variety of individual foods. In addition, frequently foods are combined. You will be able to find the TAG value of recipes without the step of matching individual foods into food groups. Analyzing a pizza by the number of bread, vegetable, meat, and fat exchanges can be confusing. The food tables in the back of the book will give you precise information on each food. Weigh the food, multiply it by the conversion factor (TAG/grams or TAG/ounce), and add up the parts. You will know exactly how much TAG is in the recipe.

Foods do not always come in exchange portions. It is frustrating to be looking at a fruit or vegetable trying to decide if the portion equals an exchange. It's back to the example of making every person in the world wear a size-6 shoe! There are times when the shoe simply does not fit. If you choose to use a portion other than the defined exchange portion, you end up using fractions. This is much more frustrating than it needs to be. As I've said earlier, you do not have to become a mathematician just because you have diabetes.

The exchange system does not offer you a quick way to convert one exchange into another. You will have a set amount of TAG to be divided as you choose among the fewer food groups of meat, milk, starch, sugar, and fat. The calorie source of recipes can be determined to assure that you are getting an appropriate amount of protein, carbohydrate, and fat while matching your TAG requirement.

The many foods that belong to each food group are similar but not identical. Through TAG you will have a precise food system that is based on the nutrient content of the specific foods that you eat.

TAG is particularly helpful during the times of year for seasonal foods. For example, tomatoes are grown in my city, Charleston, South Carolina. Anyone who lives here knows that the best tomatoes are available only for a short period of time. People eat tomatoes for breakfast, lunch, dinner, and snacks because they taste good. The dietary intervention must be realistic and inform how to select a variety of foods to satisfy nutrient requirements. It is silly to have people feel guilty when exchanging fruits, vegetables, and breads. To exchange foods should be simple! With TAG, Breakfast 1 and 2 are equal.

Breakfast 1			Breakfast 2		
2 slices bread	=	30 TAG	1½ ounces cereal	=	40 TAG
½ cup orange juice	=	14 TAG	2 ounces strawberries	=	5 TAG
1 cup milk	=	16 TAG	1 cup milk	=	16 TAG
1 egg	=	5 TAG	½ ounce almonds	=	+ 5 TAG
1 pat margarine	=	+ 1 TAG			
Total	=	66 TAG	Total	=	66 TAG

It might be convenient to consume food groups, but we actually consume specific foods. At one time my dad was on the road quite a bit with his job. He said it would be great to simply walk into a restaurant and be able to order three dollars' worth of food. It would be simple if we could purchase people chow the way we purchase dog chow. The single food would be predictable and complete. All we would have to do is individualize the amount. But, it wouldn't take much time for it to become boring!

If you learned the ADA Exchange System before 1986, you may notice changes in the food groupings. The fruit exchange has increased from 10 to 15 grams of carbohydrate. The bread/starch exchange has changed from 3 to 2 grams of protein. The estimated carbohydrate value for fruits and the protein value for breads have changed because common portions are closer to the changed amounts. The food has not changed that much. This sounds confusing! But, you will never have to wonder about common portions again if you use the conversion factors to determine the TAG value of specific amounts of food.

With the TAG food system breads, fruits, and vegetables are grouped together. You will be able to confidently increase your food options by counting a single TAG value. My hope is that your confidence will increase as you begin actively to make your food decisions.

Recipes

It is common to have fears about using recipes. Food combinations may seem complicated or difficult to fit into single food groups. The TAG value of recipes can be found for any food combination.

Food is more interesting when individual ingredients are combined as recipes. The combinations are limitless. TAG for any recipe can be determined by adding TAG of the individual ingredients. Learn how to convert your favorite recipes by following the examples.

Food tables using household measurements are provided on the following pages to facilitate the calculation of baked products. The TAG, calorie, and weight values are provided for a teaspoon, tablespoon, ¼, ⅓, ½, ⅔, ¾, and one cup. It is fine for you to use household measurements when preparing your recipes. The TAG value for ingredients used in casseroles, meat dishes, fruits, and vegetables is found in the major food tables in the back of the book.

Follow the sample recipes to discover how you can determine the TAG content of recipes that you frequently use. Most baked products simply vary the portion of flour, sugar, margarine or oil, milk products, and eggs. Spices and condiments do not contain significant TAG and therefore can be omitted from the calculations.

Consult the table to find the TAG value for the individual ingredients of the recipe. Follow the first example of a basic white-bread recipe. The ingredients are 2%-fat milk, yeast, salt, vegetable oil, white sugar, and all-purpose flour. This recipe would make one loaf of bread.

White Bread, 1 loaf (12 servings)

Ingredient	Measure		TAG
2%-fat milk	1 cup	=	17
yeast	1 tablespoon	=	5
salt	1 teaspoon (insignificant TAG)		
vegetable oil	1 tablespoon	=	1
white sugar	2 tablespoons	=	24
all-purpose flour	3 cups	=	279

TAG Values of Foods Used in Baking

Food	1 table-spoon	1/4 cup	1/3 cup	1/2 cup	2/3 cup	3/4 cup	1 cup
2%-fat milk	1	4	6	9	11	13	17
yeast	5	(unlikely to exceed 1 tablespoon)					
vegetable oil	1	6	7	11	15	17	22
white sugar	12	50	66	100	133	149	199
all-purpose flour	6	23	31	47	62	70	93

Additional tables are provided to calculate the calorie content and weight of the recipe.

Calorie Content of Foods Used in Baking

Food	1 table-spoon	1/4 cup	1/3 cup	1/2 cup	2/3 cup	3/4 cup	1 cup
2%-fat milk	8	30	40	61	81	91	121
yeast	23	(unlikely to exceed 1 tablespoon)					

Calorie Content of Foods Used in Baking

Food	1 table-spoon	¼ cup	⅓ cup	½ cup	⅔ cup	¾ cup	1 cup
vegetable oil	120	480	640	960	1280	1440	1920
white sugar	50	199	265	398	531	597	796
all-purpose flour	25	100	133	200	267	300	400

Weights (Grams) of Foods Used in Baking

Food	1 table-spoon	¼ cup	⅓ cup	½ cup	⅔ cup	¾ cup	1 cup
2%-fat milk	15	61	81	122	163	183	244
yeast	23	(unlikely to exceed 1 tablespoon)					
vegetable oil	14	56	75	112	149	168	224
white sugar	13	50	67	100	133	150	200
all-purpose flour	7	28	37	56	75	84	112

White Bread, 1 loaf (12 servings)

Ingredient	Measure	Grams	TAG	Calories
2%-fat milk	1 cup	244	17	121
yeast	1 tablespoon	23	5	23
salt	1 teaspoon	(insignificant TAG)		
vegetable oil	1 tablespoon	14	1	120
white sugar	2 tablespoons	26	24	100
all-purpose flour	3 cups	+336	+279	+1200
		643	326	1564

One loaf contains 326 TAG and 1564 calories.
One serving contains 27 TAG and 130 calories.

The amount of fat, margarine, or oil in a recipe will greatly increase calories while having a small impact on the TAG value. Fat is very high in calories (9 calories per gram) while only 10 percent of fat is converted to TAG. It is useful to estimate the percent of calories that comes from fat in recipes. Fat should provide 30–35 percent of your total calories. You can consume individual foods with a higher percent fat, but they should be eaten with low-fat foods.

The percentage of calories from fat can be estimated by dividing the high-fat calories by the total calories and multiplying by one hundred. The high-fat items are eggs, margarine, vegetable oil, and peanut butter.

White Bread, 1 loaf (12 servings)

Ingredient	Measure	Calories
2%-fat milk	1 cup	121
yeast	1 tablespoon	23
vegetable oil	1 tablespoon	120
white sugar	2 tablespoons	100
all-purpose flour	3 cups	+ 1200
		1564

Percent fat = (high-fat calories/total calories) × 100
Percent fat = (120/1564) × 100 = 8% fat

The recipe contains 120 calories from the fat in the vegetable oil. Fat equals 8 percent of the total calories. White bread is very low in fat. If you add margarine to the bread when you eat it, the fat content will increase.

Percent Fat		Fat
0–15% fat	=	very low
16–25% fat	=	low
26–35% fat	=	medium
36–45% fat	=	high
46–100% fat	=	very high

The white bread recipe can be modified to make whole-wheat bread by changing white flour to a combination of white flour and whole-wheat flour and changing white sugar to molasses.

Whole-Wheat Bread, 1 loaf (12 servings)

Ingredient	Measure	Grams	TAG	Calories
2%-fat milk	1 cup	244	17	121
salt	1 teaspoon	(insignificant TAG)		
yeast	1 tablespoon	23	5	23
vegetable oil	1 tablespoon	14	1	120
molasses	2 tablespoons	40	24	96
all-purpose flour	1½ cups	168	140	600
whole-wheat flour	1½ cups	+180	+143	+ 600
		669	330	1560

The recipe contains 330 TAG and 1560 calories.
One serving contains 38 TAG and 130 calories.

Percent fat = (120/1560) × 100 = 8% fat = very low

Biscuits differ from bread in that the fat content is much higher.

Biscuits, 12 servings

Ingredient	Measure	Grams	TAG	Calories
2%-fat milk	1 cup	244	17	121
shortening	⅓ cup	76	8	554
self-rising flour	2¼ cups	+252	+230	+ 981
		572	255	1656

The recipe contains 255 TAG and 1656 calories.
One serving contains 21 TAG and 138 calories.

Percent fat = (554/1656) × 100 = 33% fat = medium

It may be helpful to portion biscuits to be equal to a specific amount of TAG. This way you will not have to worry about trying to portion the biscuit after it has been cooked. Portioning after cooking can be confusing because baked products lose about 10 percent of their total weight during the cooking process.

The weight and TAG content of the total recipe is needed to determine the weight of food equal to a specific amount of TAG.

$$\frac{\text{Specific TAG} \times \text{recipe weight}}{\text{Recipe TAG}} = \text{weight for specific TAG}$$

The weight of the biscuit recipe is 572 grams. The recipe contains 255 TAG. A 20-TAG biscuit weighs 45 grams.

$$(20 \text{ TAG}/255 \text{ TAG}) \times 572 \text{ grams} = 45 \text{ grams per 20 TAG}$$

Perhaps you would like to know how many TAG are in a specific biscuit. Once again, you will need to know the weight and TAG value of the total recipe. Suppose your child has made a 60-gram biscuit. How many TAG would be in the biscuit?

$$\frac{\text{Specific weight} \times \text{recipe TAG}}{\text{Recipe weight}} = \text{TAG of specific weight}$$
$$(60 \text{ grams}/572 \text{ grams}) \times 255 \text{ TAG} = 27 \text{ TAG per 60 grams}$$

My mother was English, so it was common to have rock cakes for tea. Rock cakes are a cross between a biscuit and cake.

Rock Cakes, 20 servings

Ingredient	Measure	Grams	TAG	Calories
margarine	½ cup	114	12	831
white sugar	⅔ cup	133	133	531
raisins	⅔ cup	100	81	300
nutmeg	1 teaspoon	(insignificant TAG)		

Rock Cakes, 20 servings

Ingredient	Measure	Grams	TAG	Calories
self-rising flour	2½ cups	280	255	1090
2%-fat milk	½ cup	122	9	61
egg	1	+ 50	+ 5	+ 79
		799	495	2892

The recipe contains 495 TAG and 2892 calories.
One serving contains 25 TAG and 145 calories.

Percent fat = (910/2892 calories) × 100 = 31% fat = medium

How many TAG would be in a 60-gram rock cake?

$$\frac{\text{Specific weight}}{\text{Recipe weight}} \times \text{recipe TAG} = \text{TAG of specific weight}$$

(60 grams/799 grams) × 495 TAG = 37 TAG

The 60-gram rock cake contains 37 TAG while the 60-gram biscuit contains 27 TAG! The foods weigh the same but contain different amounts of TAG. The sugar content of the rock cakes is much higher. It is important to know how much sugar is in each serving. Divide the amount of TAG from sugars, molasses, or syrups by the TAG in the recipe and multiply by the TAG in each serving.

TAG in sugar group/number of servings = sugar per serving

In the rock cake recipe, 133 TAG come from sugar. There are 20 servings. One serving contains 7 grams of sugar.

133 sugar TAG/20 servings = 7 grams of sugar per serving

Most people like cookies. Unfortunately, it may be difficult to eat only one or two. Sometimes, people find it easier to eliminate all sweet foods completely. Plan ahead and you will discover the alternative of preportioning the dessert and having it with fruit.

Rolled Almond Cookies, 25 servings

Ingredient	Measure	Grams	TAG	Calories
margarine	½ cup	114	12	831
white sugar	¾ cup	150	149	597
egg	1	50	5	79
almond extract	1 teaspoon	(insignificant TAG)		
baking powder	1½ teaspoons	(insignificant TAG)		
salt	¼ teaspoon	(insignificant TAG)		
all-purpose flour	2 cups	224	186	800
2%-fat milk	1 tablespoon	+ 15	+ 1	+ 9
		553	353	2316

The recipe contains 353 TAG and 2316 calories.
One serving contains 14 TAG and 93 calories.

Percent fat = (910/2316) × 100 = 39% fat = high
Sugar per serving = 149 sugar TAG/25 servings = 6 grams

Oatmeal Raisin Cookies, 30 servings

Ingredient	Measure	Grams	TAG	Calories
white sugar	½ cup	100	100	398
brown sugar	½ cup	112	109	434
margarine	½ cup	114	12	831
egg	1	50	5	79
vanilla	1 teaspoon	(insignificant TAG)		
baking powder	½ teaspoon	(insignificant TAG)		
baking soda	½ teaspoon	(insignificant TAG)		
cinnamon	1 teaspoon	(insignificant TAG)		
all-purpose flour	1 cup	112	93	400
2%-fat milk	2 tablespoons	30	2	16
oatmeal	1 cup	84	65	333
raisins	½ cup	+ 75	+ 61	+ 225
		677	447	2716

The recipe contains 447 TAG and 2716 calories.

One serving contains 15 TAG and 91 calories.

Percent fat = (910/2716) × 100 = 34% fat = medium
Sugar per serving = 209 sugar TAG/30 servings = 7 grams

Cakes are sweeter and richer than bread or biscuits because cakes contain more sugar and eggs. Eggs are high in fat and would be used in calculating percent of calories from fat.

Yellow Cake, 12 servings

Ingredient	Measure	Grams	TAG	Calories
eggs	2	100	10	158
white sugar	1 cup	200	199	796
margarine	½ cup	114	12	831
vanilla	1 teaspoon	(insignificant TAG)		
2%-fat milk	½ cup	122	9	61
self-rising flour	2 cups	+224	+204	+ 872
		760	434	2718

The recipe contains 434 TAG and 2718 calories.
One serving contains 36 TAG and 227 calories.

Percent fat = (989/2718) × 100 = 36% fat = high
Sugar per serving = 199 sugar TAG/12 servings = 17 grams

Pound cake contains more eggs and margarine than a yellow cake.

Pound Cake, 16 servings

Ingredient	Measure	Grams	TAG	Calories
eggs	4	200	20	316
white sugar	1 cup	200	199	796
margarine	1 cup	228	23	1662
lemon juice	1 tablespoon	(insignificant TAG)		
baking powder	1 teaspoon	(insignificant TAG)		
all-purpose flour	2 cups	+224	+186	+ 800
		852	428	3574

The recipe contains 428 TAG and 3574 calories.
One serving contains 27 TAG and 223 calories.

Percent fat = (1978/3574) × 100 = 55% fat = very high
Sugar per serving = 199 sugar TAG/16 servings = 13 grams

Reduce fat by substituting "lite" margarine for regular margarine.

Pound Cake, 16 servings

Ingredient	Measure	Grams	TAG	Calories
eggs	4	200	20	316
white sugar	1 cup	200	199	796
margarine, lite	1 cup	228	17	1247
lemon juice	1 tablespoon	(insignificant TAG)		
baking powder	1 teaspoon	(insignificant TAG)		
all-purpose flour	2 cups	+224	+186	+ 800
		852	422	3159

The recipe contains 422 TAG and 3159 calories.
One serving contains 26 TAG and 197 calories.

Percent fat = (1563/3159) × 100 = 49% fat = very high
Sugar per serving = 199 sugar TAG/16 servings = 12 grams

Angel food cake is much lower in fat than many cakes because margarine and other types of fat are not used.

Angel Food, 12 servings

Ingredient	Measure	Grams	TAG	Calories
vanilla extract	1 teaspoon	(insignificant TAG)		
cream of tartar	1½ teaspoons	(insignificant TAG)		
egg whites	12	396	24	192
cake flour	1 cup	100	84	364
white sugar	¾ cup	150	149	513
powdered sugar	¾ cup	+134	+133	+ 597
		780	390	1666

The recipe contains 390 TAG and 1666 calories.
One serving contains 33 TAG and 139 calories.

Percent fat = (0/1666) × 100 = 0% fat = very low
Sugar per serving = 282 sugar TAG/12 servings = 24 grams

Gingerbread is a cake that uses molasses for sweetening. Ginger and cinnamon are added for flavor.

Gingerbread, 12 servings

Ingredient	Measure	Grams	TAG	Calories
eggs	1	50	5	79
vegetable oil	⅓ cup	75	7	640
sugar	½ cup	100	100	398
molasses	½ cup	160	96	384
baking soda	1 teaspoon	(insignificant TAG)		
ginger	1 teaspoon	(insignificant TAG)		
cinnamon	½ teaspoon	(insignificant TAG)		
boiling water	½ cup	120	0	0
all-purpose flour	1½ cups	+168	+140	+ 600
		673	348	2101

The recipe contains 348 TAG and 2101 calories.
One serving contains 29 TAG and 175 calories.

Percent fat = (719/2101) × 100 = 34% fat = medium
Sugar per serving = 196 sugar TAG/12 servings = 16 grams

This recipe can be easily modified into a raisin gingerbread by adding a cup of raisins.

Raisin Gingerbread, 16 servings

Ingredient	Measure	Grams	TAG	Calories
eggs	1	50	5	79
vegetable oil	⅓ cup	75	7	640
sugar	½ cup	100	100	398
molasses	½ cup	160	96	384

Raisin Gingerbread, 16 servings

Ingredient	Measure	Grams	TAG	Calories
raisins	1 cup	150	122	450
baking soda	1 teaspoon	(insignificant TAG)		
ginger	1 teaspoon	(insignificant TAG)		
cinnamon	½ teaspoon	(insignificant TAG)		
boiling water	½ cup	120	0	0
all-purpose flour	1½ cups	+168	+140	+ 600
		823	470	2551

The recipe contains 470 TAG and 2551 calories.
One serving contains 29 TAG and 159 calories.

$$\text{Percent fat} = (719/2551) \times 100 = 28\% \text{ fat} = \text{medium}$$
$$\text{Sugar per serving} = 196 \text{ sugar TAG}/16 \text{ servings} = 12 \text{ grams}$$

Read food labels to determine the amount of TAG in the individual ingredients of recipes. Follow the example of the vegetable soup. The recipe includes a 16-ounce can of whole tomatoes and a 16-ounce can of whole corn.

Read the label on the can of tomatoes:

16-ounce can = two 1-cup servings

one serving	= 2 grams protein	× 0.6 =	1.2 TAG
	11 grams carbohydrate	× 1.0 =	11.0 TAG
	0 grams fat	=	+ 0.0 TAG
	one serving	=	12.2 TAG
	two servings	=	24.4 TAG

Read the label on the can of corn:

16-ounce can = four ½-cup servings

one serving	= 2 grams protein	× 0.6 =	1.2 TAG
	19 grams carbohydrate	× 1.0 =	19.0 TAG
	1 gram fat	× 0.1 =	+ 0.1 TAG
	one serving	=	20.3 TAG
	four servings	=	81.2 TAG

Vegetable Soup, 5 servings

Ingredient	Measure	Grams	TAG
parsley, garlic, spices to taste		(insignificant TAG)	
whole tomatoes	1 16-ounce can	454	24
whole corn	1 16-ounce can	454	81
onion	1 medium	100	10
carrot	1 large	100	10
cauliflower	1 cup	100	7
broccoli	1 stalk	+ 100	+ 8
		1308	140

The recipe of 1308 grams contains 140 TAG.
One serving of 262 grams contains 28 TAG.

Single pieces of fruit can be boring from time to time. For variety, make a fruit salad. Simply weigh the fruits as you cut them up. The weights refer to the edible portion. Calculate the TAG from each fruit based on weight and add them up.

Fruit Salad, 15 servings

Ingredient	Grams		TAG/gm		TAG
pineapple	440	×	0.16	=	70
banana	325	×	0.24	=	78
strawberries	350	×	0.07	=	25
cantaloupe	525	×	0.09	=	47
apple	+ 275	×	0.15	=	+ 41
	1915				261

The recipe weighing 1915 grams contains 261 TAG.
One serving weighing 128 grams contains 17 TAG.

Jack's Pizza, 10 servings

Ingredient	Measure	Grams		TAG/gm		TAG
pizza crust	1 package	283	×	0.51	=	144

Jack's Pizza, 10 servings

Ingredient	Measure	Grams		TAG/gm		TAG
tomato sauce	1 4-oz. can	120	×	0.08	=	10
Parmesan	1 3-oz. package	85	×	0.27	=	23
onion	3 medium	300	×	0.10	=	30
bell pepper	1 medium	100	×	0.06	=	6
mushrooms	2 3½-oz. cans	226	×	0.06	=	14
black olives	3½-oz. can	99	×	0.06	=	6
sausage	1 pound*	300	×	0.12	=	36
shrimp	1 pound*	400	×	0.15	=	27
mozzarella	0.8 pound	369	×	0.44	=	162
pimiento	1 2-oz. jar	57	×	0.06	=	+ 3
						458

The recipe contains 458 TAG.
One serving contains 46 TAG.

*The weights of sausage and shrimp are uncooked weights. One pound (454 grams) of sausage will weigh approximately 300 grams when it is cooked and drained of excess fat.

TAG VALUES OF FOODS USED IN BAKING

Food	1 table-spoon	¼ Cup	⅓ Cup	½ Cup	⅔ Cup	¾ Cup	1 Cup
Grains							
all-purpose flour	6	23	31	47	62	70	93
barley	6	23	31	47	62	70	93
Bisquick mix	5	21	27	41	55	62	82

TAG VALUES OF FOODS USED IN BAKING

Food	1 table-spoon	¼ Cup	⅓ Cup	½ Cup	⅔ Cup	¾ Cup	1 Cup
cake flour	5	21	28	42	56	63	84
cornmeal	8	32	42	63	84	95	126
oatmeal	4	16	22	33	43	49	65
rice flour	7	28	37	56	75	84	112
rye flour	6	23	30	46	61	68	91
self-rising flour	6	26	34	51	68	77	102
whole-wheat flour	6	24	32	48	63	71	95
Dairy							
2%-fat milk	1	4	6	9	11	13	17
buttermilk	1	4	6	9	11	13	17
evaporated milk	2	9	12	18	23	26	35
skim milk	1	4	6	9	11	13	17
whole milk	1	4	6	9	11	13	17
Sweets							
brown sugar	14	54	72	109	145	163	217
chocolate chips	7	30	40	60	79	89	119
coconut, fresh	1	5	6	10	13	14	19
coconut, sweet	3	10	14	21	27	31	41
corn syrup	15	59	79	119	158	178	237
currants	7	28	37	55	73	83	110
honey	16	63	83	125	167	188	250
molasses	12	48	64	96	128	144	192
powdered sugar	11	44	59	89	118	133	177
raisins	8	31	41	61	81	92	122
white sugar	12	50	66	100	133	149	199

TAG VALUES OF FOODS USED IN BAKING

Food	1 table-spoon	¼ Cup	⅓ Cup	½ Cup	⅔ Cup	¾ Cup	1 Cup
Fats							
peanut butter	7	27	36	54	72	81	108
margarine	1	6	8	12	15	17	23
margarine, "lite"	1	4	6	9	11	13	17
shortening	1	6	8	12	15	17	23
vegetable oil	1	6	7	11	15	17	22
walnuts	2	9	12	19	25	28	37
Miscellaneous							
cocoa powder	5	21	28	42	56	63	84
yeast	5	(unlikely to exceed 1 tablespoon)					

Eggs	1	2	3	4	5	6
whole egg	5	10	15	20	25	30
egg white	2	4	6	8	10	12
egg yolk	3	6	9	12	15	18

CALORIE CONTENT OF FOODS USED IN BAKING

Food	1 table-spoon	¼ Cup	⅓ Cup	½ Cup	⅔ Cup	¾ Cup	1 Cup
Grain							
all-purpose flour	25	100	133	200	267	300	400
barley	25	100	134	201	267	301	401
Bisquick mix	30	120	160	240	320	360	480
cake flour	23	91	121	182	243	273	364
cornmeal	34	136	181	272	363	408	544
oatmeal	21	83	111	167	222	250	333

CALORIE CONTENT OF FOODS USED IN BAKING

Food	1 table-spoon	¼ Cup	⅓ Cup	½ Cup	⅔ Cup	¾ Cup	1 Cup
rice flour	30	120	160	240	319	359	479
rye flour	25	98	131	196	261	294	392
self-rising flour	27	109	145	218	291	327	436
whole-wheat flour	25	100	133	200	267	300	400
Dairy							
2%-fat milk	8	30	40	61	81	91	121
buttermilk	6	25	33	50	66	74	99
evaporated milk	19	75	100	150	200	225	300
skim milk	6	22	30	45	59	67	89
whole milk	9	38	50	75	100	113	150
Sweets							
brown sugar	54	217	289	434	579	651	868
chocolate chips	55	218	291	436	581	654	872
coconut, fresh	22	87	116	174	232	261	348
coconut, sweet	25	101	135	203	270	304	405
corn syrup	59	237	316	474	631	710	947
currants	28	113	151	227	302	340	453
honey	61	245	327	490	653	735	980
molasses	48	192	256	384	512	576	768
powdered sugar	43	171	228	342	456	513	684
raisins	28	113	150	225	300	338	450
white sugar	50	199	265	398	531	597	796
Fats							
peanut butter	92	369	492	738	983	1106	1475

CALORIE CONTENT OF FOODS USED IN BAKING

Food	1 table-spoon	1/4 Cup	1/3 Cup	1/2 Cup	2/3 Cup	3/4 Cup	1 Cup
margarine	104	416	554	831	1108	1247	1662
margarine, "lite"	78	312	416	623	831	935	1247
shortening	104	416	554	831	1108	1247	1662
vegetable oil	120	480	640	960	1280	1440	1920
walnuts	49	196	261	392	523	588	784
Miscellaneous							
cocoa powder	22	86	115	173	230	259	345
yeast	23	(unlikely to exceed 1 tablespoon)					

Eggs	1	2	3	4	5	6
whole egg	79	158	237	316	395	474
egg white	16	32	48	64	80	96
egg yolk	65	126	189	252	315	378

WEIGHTS (GRAMS) OF FOODS USED IN BAKING

Food	1 table-spoon	1/4 Cup	1/3 Cup	1/2 Cup	2/3 Cup	3/4 Cup	1 Cup
Grain							
all-purpose flour	7	28	37	56	75	84	112
barley	7	28	37	56	75	84	112
Bisquick mix	7	28	37	56	75	84	112
cake flour	6	25	33	50	67	75	100
cornmeal	9	37	50	75	99	112	149
oatmeal	5	21	28	42	56	63	84
rice flour	8	31	42	63	83	94	125

WEIGHTS (GRAMS) OF FOODS USED IN BAKING

Food	1 table-spoon	¼ Cup	⅓ Cup	½ Cup	⅔ Cup	¾ Cup	1 Cup
rye flour	7	28	37	56	75	84	112
self-rising flour	7	28	37	56	75	84	112
whole-wheat flour	8	30	40	60	80	90	120
Dairy							
2%-fat milk	15	61	81	122	163	183	244
buttermilk	15	61	82	123	163	184	245
evaporated milk	16	64	85	128	171	192	256
skim milk	15	62	82	123	164	185	246
whole milk	15	61	81	122	163	183	244
Sweets							
brown sugar	14	56	75	112	149	168	224
chocolate chips	11	42	56	84	112	126	168
coconut, fresh	6	24	32	48	64	72	96
coconut, sweet	5	21	28	42	56	63	84
corn syrup	20	80	107	160	213	240	320
currants	9	36	48	72	96	108	144
honey	20	80	107	160	213	240	320
molasses	20	80	107	160	213	240	320
powdered sugar	11	45	59	89	119	134	178
raisins	9	38	50	75	100	113	150
white sugar	13	50	67	100	133	150	200
Fats							
peanut butter	16	64	85	128	171	192	256
margarine	14	57	76	114	152	171	228

WEIGHTS (GRAMS) OF FOODS USED IN BAKING

Food	1 table-spoon	¼ Cup	⅓ Cup	½ Cup	⅔ Cup	¾ Cup	1 Cup
margarine, "lite"	14	57	76	114	152	171	228
shortening	14	57	76	114	152	171	228
vegetable oil	14	56	75	112	149	168	224
walnuts	8	32	43	64	85	96	128
Miscellaneous							
cocoa powder	7	21	28	42	56	63	84
yeast	8	(unlikely to exceed 1 tablespoon)					

Eggs	1	2	3	4	5	6
whole egg	50	100	150	200	250	300
egg white	33	66	99	132	165	198
egg yolk	17	34	51	68	85	102

Convenience Foods

Each day we make a minimum of one hundred food decisions. This includes selecting approximately twenty-five foods. For each food we also decide on portion, preparation, and finally, the timing of foods throughout the day. Making these decisions takes time. Convenience foods can be used without compromising the ability to consume a predictable amount of total available glucose.

The amount of time spent in the kitchen varies from zero, when we eat out, to hours when preparing a Thanksgiving dinner. We are busy people. Preparing meals ahead of time, frozen dinners, and fast-foods are alternatives. Also, infant foods are convenient and popular.

Frozen dinners are an alternative when you simply don't want to take the time to prepare a meal. The meals are well balanced. The portions are predictable. Minor adjustments may be needed to match your specific TAG requirement.

Lucy needs 92 TAG for supper. She has decided to have shrimp chow mein made by La Choy. By reading the label on the side of the box, you find that it contains 11.1 grams of protein, 56.1 grams of carbohydrate, and 5.6 grams of fat. This is equal to 63 TAG.

11.1 grams of protein	×	.58	=	6.4 TAG
56.1 grams of carbohydrate	×	1.00	=	56.1 TAG
5.6 grams of fat	×	.10	=	+ .6 TAG
				63.1 TAG

The number of calories can be found by multiplying the grams of protein by four, the grams of carbohydrate by four, and the grams of fat by nine. The meal contains 318 calories.

11.1 grams of protein	×	4	=	44 calories
56.1 grams of carbohydrate	×	4	=	224 calories
5.6 grams of fat	×	9	=	+ 50 calories
				318 calories

Calculating the percentage of calories from protein, carbohydrate, and fat gives you a good idea as to the type of food that you would need to add to satisfy your TAG goal. If the convenience food is high in fat, then you would select low-fat foods to balance out the needed TAG.

protein calories ÷ total calories × 100 = % protein
(44 ÷ 318) × 100 = 14% calories from protein

carbohydrate calories ÷ total calories × 100 = % carbohydrate
(224 ÷ 318) × 100 = 70% calories from carbohydrate

fat calories ÷ total calories × 100 = % fat
(50 ÷ 318) × 100 = 16% calories from fat

The shrimp chow mein dinner has a calorie distribution of 14 percent protein, 70 percent carbohydrate, and 16 percent fat. The food tables for convenience foods contain the TAG value, the calorie content, and the distribution of calories from protein, carbohydrate, and fat.

The dinner provides 63 TAG. Lucy needs to add 29 TAG to the dinner to reach the goal of 92 TAG. She could add a slice of bread (14 TAG), a pat of margarine (1 TAG) and 200 grams of milk (14 TAG).

Suppose she selected a Mexican dinner made by Banquet. That dinner provides 88 TAG. The calorie distribution is 14 percent protein, 48 percent carbohydrate, and 38 percent fat. Once again, she needs 92 TAG. The calorie distribution for the meal is appropriate. She needs 4 TAG. She could add 54 grams of strawberries to bring her total up to 92 TAG.

Fast-foods are a way of life. If you have diabetes, you do not have to exclude these foods. With information you can incorporate fast-foods wisely. With few exceptions, fast-foods are very high in fat. Without a doubt, fast-foods have contributed to Americans being 2.3 billion pounds overweight! As you study the TAG and calorie content of fast-foods, you will notice that the percent of calories from fat range from 35 percent for a roast beef sandwich to 58 percent for a bacon cheeseburger.

If you match TAG with the very high-fat foods, you will be consuming too many calories. Fat increases calories while not changing the TAG significantly. There are simple changes you can request to reduce fat and still have predictable TAG. Let people know that you do not want the mayonnaise, tartar sauce, or dressing that are so often added to these foods. The meal can be nutritious.

Enjoy the time you spend in the kitchen. By now you may be wondering if you will be spending hours in the kitchen each day planning and preparing meals. Discover alternatives that let you stay in the kitchen only as long as you want to. Simplicity is important. The meal with four items is much easier to calculate and prepare than the holiday meal with a dozen items!

Keep a file on the food combinations and corresponding portions that you like. A meal combination is calculated one time. There are so many combinations that work! Often people want me to give them a "diet sheet." It reminds me of fast-foods and convenience foods. We want things now! Allow yourself the time required to learn and apply the food system. It is similar to learning how to read. You begin with letters which lead to words and finally sentences. It takes time. Accepting the time commitment leads to a realistic approach to the food-decision process.

TAG AND CALORIE CONTENT OF FROZEN DINNERS

Food	Oz.	TAG	Calories	Protein	Carbo-hydrate	Fat
Banquet						
beans and franks	10.7	76	590	11%	43%	46%
chicken and noodles	12.0	63	370	20%	55%	25%
fish	8.7	56	380	20%	46%	34%
haddock	8.7	59	420	20%	43%	36%
ham	10.0	59	370	18%	52%	30%
Mexican	16.0	88	610	14%	48%	38%
Mexican combo	12.0	87	570	16%	51%	34%
ocean perch	8.7	63	430	18%	46%	36%
turkey	11.0	42	290	32%	38%	30%
La Choy						
almond chicken	9.8	39	290	24%	39%	38%
beef chow mein	10.8	64	340	15%	66%	18%
beef teriyaki	10.0	47	280	26%	52%	23%
chicken chow mein	11.0	44	270	27%	49%	24%
pepper oriental	10.8	65	350	16%	65%	19%
pepper steak	10.0	44	290	29%	43%	28%
shrimp chow mein	10.8	63	330	14%	70%	16%
Le Menu						
beef sirloin tips	11.5	53	420	27%	32%	40%
chicken à la king	10.2	63	490	20%	38%	42%
chicken parmigiana	11.5	46	380	28%	29%	42%
flounder fillet	10.5	42	350	25%	31%	44%
ham steak	9.9	47	320	23%	43%	33%
sliced turkey	11.2	52	450	24%	30%	46%
sweet and sour chicken	11.2	58	450	19%	38%	43%

TAG AND CALORIE CONTENT OF FROZEN DINNERS

Food	Oz.	TAG	Calories	Protein	Carbo-hydrate	Fat
Lean Cuisine						
beef, vegetable and rice	8.6	41	260	27%	45%	27%
cheese cannelloni	9.1	38	270	32%	35%	33%
chicken and vegetable	12.8	42	260	33%	43%	24%
chicken à l'orange	8.0	48	280	38%	46%	16%
chicken cacciatore	10.9	39	280	33%	35%	32%
chicken chow mein	11.2	46	250	25%	57%	18%
chicken vegetable and rice	8.5	39	270	39%	34%	27%
fish divan	12.4	36	270	45%	25%	30%
fish florentine	9.0	30	240	45%	22%	34%
fish jardinière	11.2	36	280	43%	26%	32%
linguini with clams	9.6	42	260	25%	50%	25%
meat cannelloni	9.6	36	260	27%	38%	34%
meat, tomato, cabbage	10.8	28	210	26%	36%	38%
meatball stew	10.0	34	250	35%	32%	33%
salisbury steak	9.5	30	270	37%	21%	43%
scallops, vegetable, and rice	11.0	41	220	28%	60%	13%
spaghetti with beef	11.5	47	280	22%	55%	23%
zucchini lasagna	11.0	42	260	33%	43%	24%

TAG AND CALORIE CONTENT OF FROZEN DINNERS

Food	Oz.	TAG	Calories	Protein	Carbo-hydrate	Fat
Swanson chicken,						
"hungryman"	18.9	102	730	24%	41%	36%
chicken breast, fried	11.0	68	590	22%	31%	47%
fish and chips	10.2	55	450	22%	34%	44%
ham	10.0	59	380	20%	49%	31%
lasagna	13.0	63	390	13%	55%	32%
macaroni and cheese	12.4	63	390	12%	56%	32%
Swiss steak	10.0	52	350	22%	45%	33%
turkey, three-course	16.0	80	520	20%	47%	32%
veal parmigiana	12.2	66	510	17%	39%	44%

TAG AND CALORIE CONTENT OF FAST FOODS

Food	TAG	Calories	Protein	Carbohy-drate	Fat
Arby's chicken-breast sandwich	75	590	19%	39%	42%
ham and cheese sandwich	49	350	29%	37%	33%
potato cakes	25	200	4%	40%	57%
potato, plain	71	290	11%	88%	1%
potato, deluxe	73	650	11%	36%	53%
potato with mushroom and cheese	82	540	10%	54%	37%
roast beef, junior	30	220	23%	42%	35%
roast beef, king size	62	470	24%	39%	38%
roast beef, regular	46	350	25%	36%	38%
turkey deluxe	48	380	25%	34%	41%

TAG AND CALORIE CONTENT OF FAST FOODS

Food	TAG	Calories	Protein	Carbohy-drate	Fat
Burger King					
bacon double cheeseburger	49	510	25%	21%	54%
breakfast Croissandwich	28	300	15%	27%	58%
cheeseburger	41	320	21%	37%	42%
chicken tenders	23	200	38%	19%	43%
egg platter and sausage	52	700	14%	19%	67%
french fries, regular	27	230	5%	43%	52%
french toast sticks	57	500	7%	40%	53%
"great" Danish	57	500	7%	40%	53%
hamburger	39	280	21%	41%	38%
onion rings	32	270	6%	41%	53%
scrambled egg platter	45	470	13%	29%	58%
Whaler fish sandwich	59	490	15%	36%	49%
Whopper Junior sandwich	40	320	18%	36%	46%
Whopper sandwich	65	630	18%	30%	53%
Hardee's					
apple turnover	40	280	4%	52%	44%
bacon cheeseburger	55	560	23%	24%	53%
big cookie	36	280	4%	47%	50%
big deluxe burger	52	500	23%	25%	52%
cheeseburger	44	310	18%	45%	37%
chef salad	25	280	33%	14%	52%
fisherman's fillet	64	470	21%	40%	39%
french fries, regular	31	240	5%	46%	49%
hamburger	30	280	20%	30%	50%
hot dog	35	350	13%	30%	57%
milkshake, regular	71	390	12%	64%	24%
quarter pounder	55	510	23%	28%	50%
roast beef sandwich	43	310	26%	38%	36%

TAG AND CALORIE CONTENT OF FAST FOODS

Food	TAG	Calories	Protein	Carbohy-drate	Fat
side salad	5	20	39%	58%	4%
turkey club	48	430	23%	30%	47%
Kentucky Fried Chicken					
baked beans	22	110	19%	70%	10%
buttermilk biscuits	36	270	8%	47%	45%
chicken					
breast, center, extra-crispy	32	350	30%	16%	53%
breast, side, original	23	280	29%	15%	56%
breast, side, extra-crispy	30	350	20%	20%	60%
drumstick, original	13	150	23%	6%	72%
thigh, original	24	260	40%	12%	48%
thigh, extra-crispy	28	370	21%	15%	64%
wing, original	14	180	26%	13%	61%
wing, extra-crispy	16	220	21%	14%	65%
chicken gravy	6	60	14%	30%	57%
corn on the cob	35	180	12%	73%	16%
Kentucky Nuggets, 4	16	180	25%	20%	55%
mashed potatoes	13	60	13%	78%	9%
potato salad	15	140	5%	36%	59%
McDonald's					
apple danish	56	390	6%	53%	41%
Big Mac	57	570	17%	27%	55%
Chicken McNuggets	28	320	24%	19%	57%
Egg McMuffin	43	340	22%	36%	42%
Filet-O-Fish	47	435	14%	33%	53%
french fries, regular	29	220	5%	47%	47%
hamburger	37	260	19%	43%	38%
hashbrown potatoes	16	140	4%	41%	56%
McD.L.T.	62	680	18%	24%	59%

TAG AND CALORIE CONTENT OF FAST FOODS

Food	TAG	Calories	Protein	Carbohy-drate	Fat
Quarter Pounder	51	530	23%	23%	54%
sausage biscuit	45	470	10%	30%	59%
vanilla milkshake	66	350	11%	68%	22%
Shakey's Pizza					
1/10 of 13″ pizza,					
thick crust					
cheese	33	190	24%	56%	20%
pepperoni	31	230	33%	34%	32%
sausage	33	260	32%	32%	36%
sausage mushroom	37	230	24%	52%	23%
special	34	260	32%	33%	34%
1/10 of 13″ pizza,					
thin crust					
cheese	23	140	24%	48%	27%
pepperoni	21	180	36%	23%	41%
sausage	23	210	34%	22%	44%
sausage mushroom	27	180	25%	45%	30%
special	24	210	35%	23%	42%
Taco Bell					
burrito, bean	58	350	17%	55%	28%
burrito, combination	57	400	21%	43%	36%
burrito, supreme	57	460	19%	38%	44%
enrichito	48	370	21%	38%	41%
taco	17	160	29%	22%	48%
tostada	31	180	19%	53%	28%
tostada with beef	34	290	26%	28%	46%

TAG AND CALORIE CONTENT OF INFANT FOODS

Food	Amount	Grams	Oz.	TAG	TAG/ Gram	TAG/ Oz.	Calories
Breads							
Baby cookie	1	7	0.2	5	0.71	20.1	28
Teething biscuit	1	11	0.4	9	0.84	23.0	43
Cereals							
oatmeal, dry	1 table-spoon	2.4	0.1	2	0.79	19.0	10
rice, dry	1 table-spoon	2.4	0.1	2	0.83	20.0	9
oatmeal with applesauce and banana, junior	1 jar	220	7.7	36	0.17	4.7	165
Desserts							
banana pudding	1 jar	135	4.7	17	0.13	3.7	76
Dutch apple	1 jar	220	7.7	37	0.17	4.8	151
vanilla pudding	1 jar	220	7.7	38	0.17	5.0	196
Dinners							
beef and rice	1 jar	177	6.2	21	0.12	3.4	146
chicken and noodles	1 jar	213	7.5	19	0.09	2.5	109
mixed vegetables	1 jar	213	7.5	18	0.09	2.4	71
vegetables and chicken	1 jar	213	7.5	21	0.10	2.7	106

TAG AND CALORIE CONTENT OF INFANT FOODS

Food	Amount	Grams	Oz.	TAG	TAG/ Gram	TAG/ Oz.	Calories
Fruits							
applesauce	1 jar	213	7.5	22	0.10	2.9	79
banana apple, junior	1 jar	220	7.7	40	0.18	5.1	165
peaches, junior	1 jar	220	7.7	42	0.19	5.5	157
pears and pineapple	1 jar	213	7.5	25	0.12	3.3	93
Fruit Juice							
mixed fruit	1 jar	130	4.6	15	0.12	3.3	61
orange	1 jar	130	4.6	14	0.11	3.0	58
orange-apple	1 jar	130	4.6	14	0.10	2.9	56
Meat							
beef, junior	1 jar	99	3.5	9	0.09	2.5	105
turkey, junior	1 jar	99	3.5	10	0.10	2.7	128
Milk							
2% fat	½ cup	122	4.3	9	0.07	2.0	61
skim milk	½ cup	123	4.3	9	0.07	1.9	45
whole milk	½ cup	122	4.3	9	0.07	2.0	75
Vegetables							
carrots	1 jar	213	7.5	16	0.08	2.2	67
corn, creamed	1 jar	213	7.5	37	0.17	4.9	138
green beans	1 jar	206	7.2	13	0.06	1.8	51
spinach	1 jar	213	7.5	18	0.08	2.4	90
sweet potatoes	1 jar	220	7.7	32	0.15	4.2	133

The Food Tables

The TAG value of foods is calculated from the protein, carbohydrate, and fat content of foods. *Handbook 8: Composition of Foods,* published by the U.S. Department of Agriculture, Washington, D.C., was the major reference. *Designing Foods: Animal Product Options in the Marketplace,* by the National Research Council; *Food Values of Portions Commonly Used,* by Pennington and Church; and information from food companies were also used.

The food tables that follow are divided into two groups. First, the TAG contents of foods are listed for common portions. Foods with the corresponding household measurement, weight in grams, weight in ounces, TAG, and calories are listed. Also, foods are ranked according to the percent of calories derived from fat. A blank means that the food contains 0–10 percent of the calories from fat. One star (*) means that 11–40 percent of the calories comes from fat. Two stars (**) means 41–70 percent of the calories come from fat. Three stars (***) means 71–100 percent of the calories come from fat.

The second group of tables list foods with the amount of TAG per gram and the TAG per ounce. Also, food portions in grams are listed to match 5, 10, 15, 20, 25, and 30 TAG.

With your meal plan, you can now decide on foods and corresponding portions to match your desirable TAG. The food tables are divided into the groups of meat, milk, starch, sugar, and fat.

Meat

This group includes nonmeat foods containing protein as well as meat products: beef, cheese, chicken, duck, eggs, fish, lamb, nuts, pork, turkey, and veal. The food portions refer to the cooked edible portions of the separable lean meat. Food preparation methods are detailed, as they frequently change the weight, fat, and calorie content. The weights refer to the portions as served. Raw or uncooked weights of many of the meats are listed so that you can portion the food before cooking. During the cooking process meats decrease in weight by approximately 40 percent because of water loss. If you use the uncooked weight, you do not have to reweigh the food after cooking. Use the value that is most convenient.

Milk

This is a small food group which includes milk, cottage cheese, and yogurt. You can shift the times that you have milk but do try to have two servings each day. If you have problems with low blood sugar, drink milk between meals. It supplies an excellent protein and carbohydrate combination. Milk also provides essential calcium.

Starch

This is the largest food group. It includes breads, cereals, crackers, fruit, fruit juice, grains, pasta, snacks, soups, and vegetables. These foods are high in TAG. You do not have to have a specific amount of bread, fruits, and vegetables throughout the day. During the summer, you may want more fruits and vegetables because they are in season. Be consistent with counting TAG. Variety is very important to making sure that you get all the nutrients you need.

Sugar

This food group includes beverages other than fruit juice, candy, cookies, desserts, and miscellaneous items. When planning your meal, you can switch this TAG allowance to the starch group. Do not do the reverse. If your meal plan calls for 40 TAG from starch and 15 TAG from sugar, you can have 55 TAG from starch and 0 TAG from sugar.

Fat

This includes butter, dressings, margarine, and oils. The fats are low in TAG but very high in calories. To lose weight, reduce fat.

There are lots of numbers in the food tables. Study them and you will quickly see how you can determine suitable portions to match your TAG requirement.

The tables read like mileage tables frequently found on maps. Rather than relating two cities and finding the distance, you select a food and the desired TAG to determine the portion size in grams. The food item is listed on the left. The portion in grams corresponds to a specific amount of TAG listed at the top. In addition, the "average portion" is listed with its corresponding TAG.

TAG AND CALORIE CONTENT
OF COMMON PORTIONS
Meat Group—Beef

Beef	Measure	Grams	Oz.	TAG	Calories	Fat†
beef frank	1	45	1.6	5.4	145	***
beef liver	3½ oz.	100	3.5	17.2	140	*
bottom round	3½ oz.	100	3.5	19.3	225	**
chuck blade	3½ oz.	100	3.5	19.6	275	**
corned beef	2 oz.	57	2.0	9.6	141	**
eye of round	3½ oz.	100	3.5	17.5	184	*
ground beef	3½ oz.	100	3.5	18.1	280	**
meatloaf	3½ oz.	100	3.5	15.2	160	**
rib, broiled	3½ oz.	100	3.5	16.4	233	**
roast beef	3½ oz.	100	3.5	17.4	193	*
tenderloin	3½ oz.	100	3.5	17.4	207	**

Meat Group—Cheese

Cheese	Measure	Grams	Oz.	TAG	Calories	Fat†
American	1 slice	28	1.0	5.0	107	***
American, "lite"	1 slice	28	1.0	5.9	70	**
cheddar cheese	1 slice	28	1.0	5.5	115	***
cheddar, "lite"	1 slice	28	1.0	5.9	70	**
cheese, blue	1 oz.	28	1.0	5.1	100	***
cottage, 1% fat	1 cup	226	7.9	22.7	164	*
cottage, 2% fat	1 cup	226	7.9	26.7	201	*
cream cheese	2 tbl.	28	1.0	3.0	99	***
gouda	1 slice	28	1.0	5.5	101	**
muenster	1 slice	28	1.0	5.0	105	***
muenster, "lite"	1 slice	28	1.0	5.4	53	*

† blank < 10 percent of calories from fat.
* 11–40 percent of calories from fat.
** 41–70 percent of calories from fat.
*** 71–100 percent of calories from fat.

TAG AND CALORIE CONTENT
OF COMMON PORTIONS
Meat Group—Cheese

Cheese	Measure	Grams	Oz.	TAG	Calories	Fat†
monterey jack	1 slice	28	1.0	5.1	106	***
monterey jack, "lite"	1 slice	28	1.0	4.9	51	**
mozzarella	1 slice	28	1.0	4.4	80	**
mozzarella, "lite"	1 slice	28	1.0	5.5	70	*
mozzarella, part skim	1 slice	28	1.0	5.4	69	*
Parmesan	1 slice	28	1.0	7.5	111	**
ricotta	1 slice	28	1.0	2.9	50	**
ricotta, "lite"	1 slice	28	1.0	3.7	40	**
ricotta, part skim	1 slice	28	1.0	3.6	39	**
Swiss cheese	1 slice	28	1.0	5.8	106	**
Swiss, "lite"	1 slice	28	1.0	5.9	70	**

Meat Group—Chicken

Chicken	Measure	Grams	Oz.	TAG	Calories	Fat†
breast, fried	1 medium	100	3.5	20.1	209	*
frank	1 medium	45	1.6	7.3	116	**
liver	3½ oz.	100	3.5	15.6	157	*
salad	3½ oz.	100	3.5	11.0	127	**
dark, no skin	3½ oz.	100	3.5	16.9	205	**
leg, fried	1 medium	49	1.7	9.1	120	**
light, no skin	3½ oz.	100	3.5	18.4	173	*
wing, fried	1 medium	20	0.7	4.2	54	**

† blank ≤ 10 percent of calories from fat.
* 11–40 percent of calories from fat.
** 41–70 percent of calories from fat.
*** 71–100 percent of calories from fat.

TAG AND CALORIE CONTENT
OF COMMON PORTIONS
Meat Group—Duck

Duck	Measure	Grams	Oz.	TAG	Calories	Fat†
roast, no skin	3½ oz.	100	3.5	14.8	201	**
roasted, with skin	3½ oz.	100	3.5	13.9	337	***

Meat Group—Eggs

Eggs	Measure	Grams	Oz.	TAG	Calories	Fat†
Egg Beaters	¼ cup	60	2.1	4.5	30	
eggs, boiled	1 medium	48	1.7	4.6	78	**
eggs, fried	1 medium	50	1.8	4.9	108	***
eggs, poached	1 medium	48	1.7	4.5	78	**
eggs, scrambled	1 medium	65	2.3	6.7	112	**
Scramblers	¼ cup	57	2.0	6.6	61	*

Meat Group—Fish

Fish	Measure	Grams	Oz.	TAG	Calories	Fat†
catfish, raw	3½ oz.	100	3.5	10.5	103	*
crab cake	3½ oz.	100	3.5	13.0	155	**
crab, steamed	3½ oz.	100	3.5	11.9	102	*
fishsticks	4–5	100	3.5	17.0	176	**
haddock, fried	3½ oz.	100	3.5	19.7	205	**
haddock, broiled	3½ oz.	100	3.5	14.1	112	
halibut, fried	3½ oz.	100	3.5	20.9	226	**
halibut, broiled	3½ oz.	100	3.5	15.8	140	*
oysters, fried	3½ oz.	100	3.5	18.0	197	**

† blank ≤ 10 percent of calories from fat.
* 11–40 percent of calories from fat.
** 41–70 percent of calories from fat.
*** 71–100 percent of calories from fat.

TAG AND CALORIE CONTENT
OF COMMON PORTIONS
Meat Group—Fish

Fish	Measure	Grams	Oz.	TAG	Calories	Fat†
oysters, canned	3½ oz.	100	3.5	8.3	69	*
perch	3½ oz.	100	3.5	11.4	91	
red snapper	3½ oz.	100	3.5	11.6	93	
salmon, Atlantic	3½ oz.	100	3.5	14.4	217	**
salmon, pink	3½ oz.	100	3.5	12.0	119	*
scallops, fried	3½ oz.	100	3.5	21.7	215	**
scallops, steamed	3½ oz.	100	3.5	15.4	112	
shrimp in shell	¼ pound	114	4.0	9.5	61	
shrimp, fried	3½ oz.	100	3.5	25.1	242	**
shrimp, steamed	3½ oz.	100	3.5	15.4	112	
tuna salad	½ cup	100	3.5	13.0	170	**
tuna, oil-packed	3½ oz.	100	3.5	17.7	199	*
tuna, water-packed	3½ oz.	100	3.5	15.7	136	*

Meat Group—Lamb

Lamb	Measure	Grams	Oz.	TAG	Calories	Fat†
blade, roasted	3½ oz.	100	3.5	16.8	229	**
leg-sirloin	3½ oz.	100	3.5	18.4	221	**
loin chop, broiled	3½ oz.	100	3.5	18.3	221	**

† blank ≤ 10 percent of calories from fat.
* 11–40 percent of calories from fat.
** 41–70 percent of calories from fat.
*** 71–100 percent of calories from fat.

TAG AND CALORIE CONTENT
OF COMMON PORTIONS
Meat Group—Nuts

Nuts	Measure	Grams	Oz.	TAG	Calories	Fat†
almonds	12–15	15	0.5	5.3	90	***
Brazil nuts	4 medium	15	0.5	4.0	97	***
cashews	6–8	15	0.5	6.6	84	**
hazelnuts	10–12	15	0.5	4.9	97	***
peanut butter	1 tbl.	15	0.5	6.3	86	**
peanuts	1 oz.	28	1.0	11.0	152	**
peanuts in shell	1 oz. EP	37	1.3	11.0	152	**
pecans	12 halves	15	0.5	3.9	104	***
sunflower seeds	1 oz.	28	1.0	10.0	172	***
sunflower in hulls	1 oz. EP	57	2.0	10.0	172	***
walnuts	8–15	15	0.5	4.6	98	***

Meat Group—Pork

Pork	Measure	Grams	Oz.	TAG	Calories	Fat†
bacon bits	1 tbl.	9	0.3	4.7	38	*
bacon, Canadian	1 slice	10	0.4	1.5	19	*
bacon, fried	1 slice	6	0.2	1.4	35	***
bologna	1 slice	28	1.0	3.1	88	***
ham, 5% fat	3½ oz.	100	3.5	12.7	145	*
ham, 11% fat	3½ oz.	100	3.5	14.0	178	**
pepperoni	1 slice	28	1.0	3.8	73	***
picnic ham	3½ oz.	100	3.5	20.0	248	**
pork chop, lean	1	68	2.4	14.4	170	**
potted meats	1 oz.	28	1.0	3.4	69	***
salami	1 slice	28	1.0	3.8	73	***
sausage, pork	1 pattie	28	1.0	3.3	97	***

† blank ≤ 10 percent of calories from fat.
* 11–40 percent of calories from fat.
** 41–70 percent of calories from fat.
*** 71–100 percent of calories from fat.

TAG AND CALORIE CONTENT
OF COMMON PORTIONS
Meat Group—Turkey

Turkey	Measure	Grams	Oz.	TAG	Calories	Fat†
dark, no skin	3½ oz.	100	3.5	17.3	187	*
dark with skin	3½ oz.	100	3.5	17.1	221	**
light, no skin	3½ oz.	100	3.5	17.7	157	*
light with skin	3½ oz.	100	3.5	17.4	197	**
turkey frank	1	45	1.6	4.8	100	***

Meat Group—Veal

Veal	Measure	Grams	Oz.	TAG	Calories	Fat†
cutlet, fried	3½ oz.	100	3.5	19.4	178	*
sirloin, braised	3½ oz.	100	3.5	19.4	178	*

Milk Group

Milk	Measure	Grams	Oz.	TAG	Calories	Fat†
2%-fat milk	1 cup	244	8.6	16.9	122	*
buttermilk	1 cup	245	8.6	16.6	99	*
Cambridge diet	for day	100	3.5	64.4	339	
chocolate 2%						
fat	1 cup	250	8.8	31.1	179	*
eggnog	1 cup	254	8.9	41.9	342	**
evaporated milk	1 cup	256	9.0	40.0	200	
malted milk	1 cup	265	9.3	33.9	236	*
nonfat dry milk	¼ cup	30	1.1	21.9	109	
skim milk	1 cup	246	8.6	16.6	89	
whole milk	1 cup	244	8.6	17.0	150	**
yogurt, fruit	1 cup	227	8.0	47.8	225	
yogurt, plain	1 cup	227	8.0	23.2	143	*

† blank ≤ 10 percent of calories from fat.
* 11–40 percent of calories from fat.
** 41–70 percent of calories from fat.
*** 71–100 percent of calories from fat.

TAG AND CALORIE CONTENT
OF COMMON PORTIONS
Starch Group—Breads

Bread	Measure	Grams	Oz.	TAG	Calories	Fat†
bagel	1 medium	55	1.9	34.5	163	
biscuits	1 medium	35	1.2	18.2	130	**
bread crumbs	1 cup	88	3.1	71.4	345	
bread, "lite"	1 slice	22	0.8	9.2	40	
breadsticks	1	6	0.2	4.9	23	
cornbread	1 piece	45	1.6	15.3	93	*
doughnuts	1 medium	30	1.1	13.2	124	**
French bread	1 slice	25	0.9	14.1	70	
French toast	1 slice	65	2.3	21.2	153	*
hamburger bun	1 medium	40	1.4	22.3	114	*
hot dog bun	1 medium	42	1.5	22.3	116	*
muffin						
blueberry	1 medium	40	1.4	21.3	126	*
bran	1 medium	40	1.4	19.0	112	*
English	1 medium	57	2.0	28.9	135	
pancakes/						
waffles	2	90	3.2	35.0	208	*
pizza crust	1	283	9.9	144.5	720	
rolls	1 medium	28	1.0	16.9	92	*
rye bread	1 slice	25	0.9	13.3	66	
sourdough						
bread	1 slice	28	1.0	14.9	68	
sweet roll	1 medium	55	1.9	30.3	174	*
taco shell	1 medium	11	0.4	8.0	50	*
tortilla, corn	1 medium	30	1.1	14.1	67	
tortilla, flour	1 medium	30	1.1	18.9	95	*
white bread	1 slice	23	0.8	12.8	62	
whole-wheat						
bread	1 slice	23	0.8	12.5	56	

† blank ≤ 10 percent of calories from fat.
* 11–40 percent of calories from fat.
** 41–70 percent of calories from fat.
*** 71–100 percent of calories from fat.

TAG AND CALORIE CONTENT
OF COMMON PORTIONS
Starch Group—Cereals

Cereal	Measure	Grams	Oz.	TAG	Calories	Fat†
All-Bran	½ cup	35	1.2	16.4	90	
All-Bran, extra fiber	½ cup	28	1.0	10.8	60	*
Bran Chex	⅔ cup	28	1.0	24.4	91	
bran flakes	¾ cup	28	1.0	24.4	92	
bran, 100%	½ cup	28	1.0	22.9	76	
Cheerios	1¼ cups	28	1.0	22.3	111	
corn bran	⅔ cup	28	1.0	25.1	98	
Corn Chex	1 cup	28	1.0	26.1	111	
cornflakes	1 cup	28	1.0	25.6	110	
Cream of Wheat	¾ cup	188	6.6	22.5	100	
Fruit & Fibre	½ cup	28	1.0	23.6	87	
granola	⅓ cup	28	1.0	21.1	126	*
Grape-Nuts	¼ cup	28	1.0	25.1	101	
Most	⅔ cup	28	1.0	24.0	95	
oat flakes	⅔ cup	28	1.0	23.6	105	
oatmeal, cooked	¾ cup	175	6.2	21.7	108	*
oatmeal, dry	⅓ cup	28	1.0	21.8	111	*
Product 19	¾ cup	28	1.0	25.1	108	
Raisin Bran	¾ cup	38	1.3	33.2	120	
Ralston	¾ cup	190	6.7	23.7	100	
Rice Krispies	1 cup	28	1.0	25.9	112	
shredded wheat	1 oz.	28	1.0	24.5	102	
Special K	1⅓ cups	28	1.0	24.6	111	
Total	1 cup	28	1.0	24.0	100	
wheat germ	3 tbl.	28	1.0	15.5	110	*
Wheaties	1 cup	28	1.0	24.2	99	

† blank ≤ 10 percent of calories from fat.
* 11–40 percent of calories from fat.
** 41–70 percent of calories from fat.
*** 71–100 percent of calories from fat.

TAG AND CALORIE CONTENT
OF COMMON PORTIONS
Starch Group—Crackers

Crackers	Measure	Grams	Oz.	TAG	Calories	Fat†
cheese crackers	5 pieces	15	0.5	9.1	81	**
graham crackers	2 squares	14	0.5	11.1	54	*
Hi Ho	4	16	0.6	10.6	82	**
melba toast	1	4	0.1	3.0	15	
saltines	2	6	0.2	5.0	28	*
Wheat Thins	4	7	0.2	5.4	36	*

Starch Group—Grains

Grain	Measure	Grams	Oz.	TAG	Calories	Fat†
barley	3½ oz.	100	3.5	83.7	349	
grits, cooked	1 cup	242	8.5	33.5	146	
grits, dry	3 tbl.	30	1.1	24.9	109	
rice, brown	⅘ cup	150	5.3	40.5	178	
rice, white	⅘ cup	150	5.3	38.1	164	
rice, dry	1 oz.	28	1.0	23.9	130	

Starch Group—Pasta

Pasta	Measure	Grams	Oz.	TAG	Calories	Fat†
macaroni and cheese	½ cup	100	3.5	37.1	245	*
noodles, cooked	⅗ cup	92	3.2	22.5	107	
pasta, dry	1 oz.	28	1.0	23.9	130	
spaghetti, cooked	1 cup	146	5.1	48.3	216	

† blank ≤ 10 percent of calories from fat.
* 11–40 percent of calories from fat.
** 41–70 percent of calories from fat.
*** 71–100 percent of calories from fat.

TAG AND CALORIE CONTENT
OF COMMON PORTIONS
Starch Group—Snacks

Snack	Measure	Grams	Oz.	TAG	Calories	Fat†
corn chips	1 oz.	28	1.0	20.1	135	**
granola bar	1 bar	24	0.8	17.8	117	*
peanut butter and cheese cracker	1 package	39	1.4	23.6	190	**
pizza, cheese	¼ small	133	4.7	45.8	320	*
pizza, cheese and meat	¼	165	5.8	45.2	367	**
popcorn, no butter	1 cup	14	0.5	11.8	54	
potato chips	1 oz.	28	1.0	18.4	144	**
pretzels	1 oz.	28	1.0	24.0	111	

Starch Group—Soups

Soup	Measure	Grams	Oz.	TAG	Calories	Fat†
asparagus/ water	1 cup	244	8.6	12.4	87	**
bean with bacon	1 cup	253	8.9	28.0	173	*
beef broth	1 cup	240	8.4	1.7	16	*
black bean	1 cup	247	8.7	23.2	116	
chicken broth	1 cup	244	8.6	3.9	39	*
chicken chunky	1 cup	251	8.8	25.3	178	*
chicken noodle	1 cup	241	8.5	12.0	75	*
chicken and rice	1 cup	241	8.5	9.4	60	*
chili con carne	1 cup	250	8.8	42.9	333	**
lentil with ham	1 cup	248	8.7	25.9	140	*
mushroom/ milk	1 cup	248	8.7	19.9	203	**

† blank ≤ 10 percent of calories from fat.
* 11–40 percent of calories from fat.
** 41–70 percent of calories from fat.
*** 71–100 percent of calories from fat.

TAG AND CALORIE CONTENT
OF COMMON PORTIONS
Starch Group—Soups

Soup	Measure	Grams	Oz.	TAG	Calories	Fat†
mushroom/ water	1 cup	244	8.6	11.5	129	**
oyster/milk	1 cup	241	8.5	5.7	59	**
pea with milk	1 cup	254	8.9	40.2	239	*
pea with water	1 cup	250	8.8	31.8	164	*
spaghetti and meat sauce	10 oz.	292	10.3	48.8	396	**
tomato with milk	1 cup	248	8.7	26.4	160	*
tomato with water	1 cup	244	8.6	18.0	86	*
turkey vegetable	1 cup	241	8.5	10.7	74	*
vegetable beef	1 cup	244	8.6	13.6	79	*
vegetable beef stew	1 cup	240	8.4	26.9	171	*
vegetable, chunky	1 cup	240	8.4	21.4	122	*
vegetarian vegetable	1 cup	241	8.5	13.4	72	*

Starch Group—Fruits

Fruit	Measure	Grams	Oz.	TAG	Calories	Fat†
apple	1 medium	138	4.9	20.2	81	
apple with core	1 medium	174	6.1	20.2	81	
applesauce	½ cup	122	4.3	13.2	53	
apricots	3 medium	106	3.7	12.7	51	
apricots, dry	10 halves	35	1.2	22.4	83	

† blank ≤ 10 percent of calories from fat.
* 11–40 percent of calories from fat.
** 41–70 percent of calories from fat.
*** 71–100 percent of calories from fat.

TAG AND CALORIE CONTENT
OF COMMON PORTIONS
Starch Group—Fruits

Fruit	Measure	Grams	Oz.	TAG	Calories	Fat†
banana	1 medium	114	4.0	27.5	105	
banana with peel	1 medium	182	6.4	27.5	105	
blackberries	1 cup	144	5.1	19.0	74	
blueberries	1 cup	145	5.1	21.1	82	
cantaloupe	1 cup	160	5.6	14.3	57	
cantaloupe with skin	1 cup	381	13.4	14.3	57	
cherries	10	68	2.4	11.8	49	
cherries with stones	10	92	3.2	11.8	49	
cranberries	1 cup	95	3.3	12.4	46	
cranberry sauce	¼ cup	69	2.4	26.9	105	
currants	1 cup	144	5.1	110.0	453	
dates	10	83	2.9	62.0	228	
dates with pit	10	96	3.4	62.0	228	
elderberries	1 cup	145	5.1	27.4	105	
figs	2 medium	100	3.5	18.5	74	
fruit cocktail	½ cup	124	4.4	15.1	56	
gooseberries	1 cup	150	5.3	16.1	67	
grapefruit	½ medium	123	4.3	9.9	37	
grapefruit with skin	½ medium	185	6.5	9.9	37	
grapes	1 cup	92	3.2	15.5	58	
honeydew melon	1 cup	170	6.0	16.1	60	

† blank ≤ 10 percent of calories from fat.
* 11–40 percent of calories from fat.
** 41–70 percent of calories from fat.
*** 71–100 percent of calories from fat.

TAG AND CALORIE CONTENT
OF COMMON PORTIONS
Starch Group—Fruits

Fruit	Measure	Grams	Oz.	TAG	Calories	Fat†
kiwifruit	1 medium	76	2.7	11.8	46	
mango	1 medium	207	7.3	35.9	135	
nectarine	1 medium	136	4.8	17.2	67	
orange	1 medium	140	4.9	17.1	65	
mandarin	½ cup	124	4.4	12.4	46	
navel with skin	1 medium	188	6.6	17.1	65	
valencia with skin	1	120	4.2	17.1	65	
papaya	1 medium	304	10.7	30.9	117	
peach	1 medium	87	3.1	9.5	37	
peach with pit	1 medium	100	3.5	9.5	37	
peaches, canned	½ cup	124	4.4	14.9	55	
pear	1 medium	166	5.8	25.5	98	
pear with core	1 medium	177	6.2	25.5	98	
persimmons	4 medium	100	3.5	34.1	128	
pineapple, juice-packed	1 cup	250	8.8	39.8	150	
plum	1 medium	66	2.3	8.9	36	
plum with pit	1 medium	76	2.7	8.9	36	
prunes with pit	10 dry EP	93	3.3	52.3	201	
prunes, dry	10	84	3.0	52.3	201	
raisins	⅔ cup	100	3.5	78.9	289	
raspberries	1 cup	123	4.3	14.9	61	
strawberries	1 cup	149	5.2	10.3	45	
tangelo	1 medium	170	6.0	9.5	39	
tangerine	1 medium	84	3.0	9.7	37	

† blank ≤ 10 percent of calories from fat.
* 11–40 percent of calories from fat.
** 41–70 percent of calories from fat.
*** 71–100 percent of calories from fat.

TAG AND CALORIE CONTENT
OF COMMON PORTIONS
Starch Group—Fruits

Fruit	Measure	Grams	Oz.	TAG	Calories	Fat†
tangerine with skin	1 medium	109	3.8	9.7	37	
watermelon	1 cup	160	5.6	12.2	50	
watermelon with skin	1 cup	420	14.8	12.2	50	

Starch Group—Fruit Juice

Fruit Juice	Measure	Grams	Oz.	TAG	Calories	Fat†
apple juice	1 cup	248	8.7	29.2	116	
cranberry juice	1 cup	253	8.9	37.8	147	
grape juice	1 cup	253	8.9	38.7	155	
grapefruit juice	1 cup	247	8.7	23.8	93	
lime juice	1 tbl.	15	0.5	1.0	4	
orange juice	1 cup	249	8.8	25.4	104	
orange/ grapefruit juice	1 cup	247	8.7	24.6	99	
pineapple juice	1 cup	250	8.8	34.9	139	
prune juice	1 cup	256	9.0	45.6	181	
tomato juice	1 cup	243	8.5	11.1	41	
V-8 juice	1 cup	242	8.5	11.5	53	

Starch Group—Vegetables

Vegetable	Measure	Grams	Oz.	TAG	Calories	Fat†
artichoke	1 large	100	3.5	11.5	44	
asparagus	⅔ cup	100	3.5	4.9	20	
avocado	1 medium	173	6.1	17.1	306	***

† blank ≤ 10 percent of calories from fat.
* 11–40 percent of calories from fat.
** 41–70 percent of calories from fat.
*** 71–100 percent of calories from fat.

TAG AND CALORIE CONTENT
OF COMMON PORTIONS
Starch Group—Vegetables

Vegetable	Measure	Grams	Oz.	TAG	Calories	Fat†
avocado with seed	1 medium	231	8.1	17.1	306	***
bean sprouts	1 cup	82	2.9	4.3	23	
beans and chili	1 cup	260	9.1	51.8	240	
beans, white, cooked	½ cup	100	3.5	25.8	118	
beets, sliced	⅗ cup	100	3.5	6.7	27	
blackeye peas	½ cup	80	2.8	18.3	86	
broccoli	1 stalk	100	3.5	6.5	32	
Brussel sprouts	6–8 medium	100	3.5	8.9	36	
cabbage, cooked	⅗ cup	100	3.5	5.0	20	
carrots, cooked	⅔ cup	100	3.5	7.6	31	
cauliflower	1 cup	100	3.5	6.8	27	
celery, raw	1 stalk	50	1.8	2.2	8	
chard, cooked	⅗ cup	100	3.5	4.4	18	
coleslaw	1 cup	120	4.2	8.4	173	***
collards, cooked	½ cup	100	3.5	6.5	29	
corn on cob	1 small ear	114	4.0	15.1	60	
corn, cooked	⅗ cup	100	3.5	16.9	66	
corn, creamed	⅖ cup	100	3.5	19.7	73	
cucumbers	½ medium	50	1.8	2.0	8	

† blank ≤ 10 percent of calories from fat.
* 11–40 percent of calories from fat.
** 41–70 percent of calories from fat.
*** 71–100 percent of calories from fat.

TAG AND CALORIE CONTENT OF COMMON PORTIONS
Starch Group—Vegetables

Vegetable	Measure	Grams	Oz.	TAG	Calories	Fat†
eggplant, cooked	½ cup	100	3.5	4.7	19	
green beans	⅔ cup	100	3.5	3.7	15	
greens, mustard	½ cup	100	3.5	5.3	23	
kale, cooked	¾ cup	100	3.5	5.9	28	
kidney beans, canned	⅖ cup	100	3.5	19.8	90	
leeks	3–4 medium	100	3.5	12.5	52	
lentils, cooked	⅔ cup	100	3.5	23.8	106	
lettuce, iceberg	3½ oz.	100	3.5	3.2	14	
lima beans, baby	½ cup	95	3.3	28.6	128	
lima beans	⅝ cup	100	3.5	24.3	111	
mixed vegetables	⅔ cup	100	3.5	12.8	60	
mushrooms, raw	10 small	100	3.5	6.0	37	
okra, cooked	8–9 pods	100	3.5	7.2	29	
olives, black	1 large	20	0.7	1.1	37	***
olives, green	2 medium	13	0.5	0.5	16	***
onions, raw	1 medium	100	3.5	9.6	38	
parsnips	½ cup	100	3.5	15.8	66	
peas and carrots	⅗ cup	100	3.5	9.7	45	
peas, frozen	⅗ cup	100	3.5	17.5	81	
peppers, green	1 large	100	3.5	5.5	22	
pickle relish	1 tbl.	15	0.5	5.2	21	
pickle, dill	1 large	100	3.5	2.6	11	

† blank ≤ 10 percent of calories from fat.
* 11–40 percent of calories from fat.
** 41–70 percent of calories from fat.
*** 71–100 percent of calories from fat.

TAG AND CALORIE CONTENT
OF COMMON PORTIONS
Starch Group—Vegetables

Vegetable	Measure	Grams	Oz.	TAG	Calories	Fat†
pickle, sweet	1 large	100	3.5	37.0	146	
pimiento	3 medium	100	3.5	6.4	27	
pork and beans, canned	½ cup	130	4.6	27.9	125	
potatoes						
au gratin	⅔ cup	100	3.5	16.6	150	**
baked	1 medium	100	3.5	22.6	95	
boiled	1 medium	100	3.5	18.3	76	
fries	¾ cup	85	3.0	21.9	138	*
frozen	¾ cup	85	3.0	21.9	138	*
mashed	½ cup	100	3.5	14.0	94	*
salad	½ cup	125	4.4	20.2	181	**
sweet	1 small	100	3.5	33.8	141	
pumpkin	⅖ cup	100	3.5	8.5	33	
radish	10 small	100	3.5	4.2	17	
rhubarb, raw	1 cup	137	4.8	7.5	29	
rutabagas	½ cup	100	3.5	8.7	35	
salad, three bean	⅖ cup	100	3.5	17.8	75	
salad, tossed	1 cup	100	3.5	4.3	18	
sauerkraut	⅔ cup	100	3.5	5.1	21	
snow peas	½ cup	84	3.0	10.7	45	
soybeans	½ cup	100	3.5	17.8	130	*
spinach, cooked	½ cup	90	3.2	5.9	21	
squash	½ cup	100	3.5	4.9	19	
tofu, soybean curd	½ cup	100	3.5	7.3	72	**
tomato paste	1 cup	262	9.2	54.0	215	

† blank ≤ 10 percent of calories from fat.
* 11–40 percent of calories from fat.
** 41–70 percent of calories from fat.
*** 71–100 percent of calories from fat.

TAG AND CALORIE CONTENT
OF COMMON PORTIONS
Starch Group—Vegetables

Vegetable	Measure	Grams	Oz.	TAG	Calories	Fat†
tomato sauce	⅖ cup	100	3.5	8.1	31	
tomatoes	1 small	100	3.5	5.4	22	
tomatoes, canned	⅖ cup	100	3.5	5.0	21	
turnips, cooked	⅔ cup	100	3.5	5.4	23	
water chestnuts	3 small	15	0.5	6.5	29	
zucchini	½ cup	95	3.3	4.0	16	

Sugar Group—Beverages

Beverage	Measure	Grams	Oz.	TAG	Calories	Fat†
beer	1 can	360	12.7	14.3	160	
beer, "lite"	1 can	360	12.7	13.0	134	
coffee	Free					
coffee, decaf	Free					
Gatorade	1 cup	230	8.1	10.5	39	
whiskey	1.6 oz.	45	1.6	2.0	133	
Kool-Aid	1 cup	240	8.4	25.0	100	
lemonade	1 cup	246	8.6	23.9	94	
limeade	1 cup	240	8.4	26.9	100	
soda, diet	Free					
soda, sweet	1 can	360	12.7	36.0	144	
tea	Free					
wine	½ cup	120	4.2	5.1	102	

Sugar Group—Candy

Candy	Measure	Grams	Oz.	TAG	Calories	Fat†
Almond Joy	1 oz.	28	1.0	20.3	151	**
caramel	3 pieces	28	1.0	20.7	120	*

† blank ≤ 10 percent of calories from fat.
* 11–40 percent of calories from fat.
** 41–70 percent of calories from fat.
*** 71–100 percent of calories from fat.

TAG AND CALORIE CONTENT
OF COMMON PORTIONS
Sugar Group—Candy

Candy	Measure	Grams	Oz.	TAG	Calories	Fat†
chewing gum	1 stick	3	0.1	2.3	10	
chewing gum, diet	1 stick	Free				
chocolate candy	1.02 oz.	29	1.0	18.7	160	**
Fruit and Nut	1 oz.	28	1.0	18.3	152	**
hard candy	6 pieces	28	1.0	27.2	108	
Kit Kat	1.13 oz.	32	1.1	21.1	162	**
Life Savers	5 pieces	10	0.4	9.7	39	
M & M's, peanut	1.67 oz.	47	1.7	32.1	240	**
M & M's, plain	1.59 oz.	45	1.6	33.7	220	*
marshmallow	1 large	8	0.3	6.3	25	
Milky Way	2.1 oz.	60	2.1	45.6	260	*
Mounds	1 oz.	28	1.0	21.3	147	**
Nestle's Crunch	1.06 oz.	30	1.1	21.0	160	**
Snickers	2 oz.	57	2.0	37.8	270	**
3 Musketeers	2.28 oz.	65	2.3	51.0	280	*
Twix	1.73 oz.	49	1.7	17.2	120	**

Sugar Group—Cookies

Cookies	Measure	Grams	Oz.	TAG	Calories	Fat†
Animal Crackers	15	28	1.0	23.4	120	*
chocolate chip	1 medium	10	0.4	7.0	46	**
fig bar	1 medium	14	0.5	11.0	53	*
oatmeal	1 medium	18	0.6	13.2	80	*
sandwich	1 medium	14	0.5	10.4	69	*
sugar-butter	1 medium	20	0.7	14.6	89	*

† blank ≤ 10 percent of calories from fat.
* 11–40 percent of calories from fat.
** 41–70 percent of calories from fat.
*** 71–100 percent of calories from fat.

TAG AND CALORIE CONTENT
OF COMMON PORTIONS
Sugar Group—Desserts

Dessert	Measure	Grams	Oz.	TAG	Calories	Fat†
cake						
angel food	1 piece	60	2.1	38.5	161	
devil's food	1 piece	60	2.1	27.4	191	**
pound	1 piece	60	2.1	31.9	284	**
yellow	1 piece	75	2.6	42.6	283	*
frozen yogurt	½ cup	113	4.0	23.0	108	
gelatin	½ cup	140	4.9	19.6	81	
ice cream	1 cup	133	4.7	35.9	257	**
ice cream,						
diabetic	1 cup	131	4.6	31.8	249	**
ice milk	1 cup	131	4.6	32.6	184	*
pie, apple	⅛	118	4.1	45.6	282	*
pie, pumpkin	⅙	95	3.3	35.1	206	*
sherbet	1 cup	193	6.8	60.4	270	
Twinkies	2 cakes	84	3.0	51.2	286	*
pudding						
sugarfree	½ cup	145	5.1	15.6	90	*
tapioca	½ cup	105	3.7	20.6	133	*
vanilla	½ cup	148	5.2	33.6	147	

Sugar Group—Miscellaneous

Miscellaneous	Measure	Grams	Oz.	TAG	Calories	Fat†
apple butter	1 tbl.	20	0.7	9.0	37	
BBQ sauce	1 tbl.	16	0.6	1.5	15	*
creamer, whip	1 tbl.	14	0.5	2.2	22	**
creamer,						
nondairy	1 tsp.	2	0.1	1.2	11	

† blank ≤ 10 percent of calories from fat.
* 11–40 percent of calories from fat.
** 41–70 percent of calories from fat.
*** 71–100 percent of calories from fat.

TAG AND CALORIE CONTENT
OF COMMON PORTIONS
Sugar Group—Miscellaneous

Miscellaneous	Measure	Grams	Oz.	TAG	Calories	Fat†
Equal	Free					
honey	1 tbl.	20	0.7	16.6	61	
jam-jellies	1 tbl.	20	0.7	14.3	55	
jelly, low- calorie	Free					
ketchup	1 tbl.	15	0.5	4.0	16	
mustard	1 tsp.	5	0.2	0.4	4	
sugar	1 tbl.	12	0.4	11.9	48	
sugar, brown	1 tbl.	14	0.5	13.4	54	
syrup, chocolate	2 tbl.	28	1.0	17.0	73	
syrup, "lite"	1 tbl.	15	0.5	4.0	16	
syrup, pancake	1 tbl.	20	0.7	14.8	57	
vinegar	Free					

Fat Group

Fat	Measure	Grams	Oz.	TAG	Calories	Fat†
dressings						
1000 Island	1 tbl.	14	0.5	3.0	70	***
French	1 tbl.	14	0.5	3.0	57	***
French, low- calorie	1 tbl.	16	0.6	3.6	22	*
Italian	1 tbl.	14	0.5	1.8	77	***
gravies						
brown	¼ cup	72	2.5	10.1	164	***
milk	¼ cup	72	2.5	10.1	164	***
white sauce	2 tbl.	33	1.2	4.3	54	**

† blank ≤ 10 percent of calories from fat.
* 11–40 percent of calories from fat.
** 41–70 percent of calories from fat.
*** 71–100 percent of calories from fat.

TAG AND CALORIE CONTENT
OF COMMON PORTIONS
Fat Group

Fat	Measure	Grams	Oz.	TAG	Calories	Fat†
spreads						
butter, stick	1 tbl.	15	0.5	1.3	108	***
butter,						
whipped	1 tbl.	11	0.4	1.0	81	***
margarine	1 tbl.	15	0.5	1.3	108	***
margarine,						
diet	1 tbl.	15	0.5	1.4	51	***
mayonnaise	1 tbl.	14	0.5	1.5	101	***
mayonnaise,						
diet	1 tbl.	15	0.5	2.7	35	**
vegetable oil	1 tbl.	14	0.5	1.4	124	***

TAG FACTORS—FOOD WEIGHTS TO TAG
Meat Group—Beef

Beef	TAG/ gram	TAG/ oz.	Grams of Food Equal to TAG					
			5	10	15	20	25	30
beef frank	0.12	3.4	42	84	126	167	209	251
beef liver	0.17	4.9	29	58	87	116	145	174
bottom round	0.19	5.5	26	52	78	103	129	155
chuck blade	0.20	5.6	25	51	76	102	127	153
corned beef	0.17	4.8	30	60	89	119	149	179
eye of round	0.18	5.0	29	57	86	114	143	172
ground beef	0.18	5.2	28	55	83	110	138	166
meat loaf	0.15	4.3	33	66	99	132	164	197
rib, broiled	0.16	4.7	30	61	91	122	152	182
tenderloin	0.17	5.0	29	58	86	115	144	173
roast beef	0.17	5.0	29	57	86	115	143	172

† blank ≤ 10 percent of calories from fat.
* 11–40 percent of calories from fat.
** 41–70 percent of calories from fat.
*** 71–100 percent of calories from fat.

TAG FACTORS—FOOD WEIGHTS TO TAG
Meat Group—Cheese

Cheese	TAG/ gram	TAG/ oz.	Grams of Food Equal to TAG					
			5	10	15	20	25	30
American	0.18	5.0	28	56	83	111	139	167
American, "lite"	0.21	5.9	24	48	71	95	119	143
cheddar	0.20	5.5	26	51	77	103	128	154
cheddar, "lite"	0.21	5.9	24	48	71	95	119	143
cheese, blue	0.18	5.1	28	55	83	111	138	166
cottage 1% fat	0.10	2.9	50	100	150	199	249	299
cottage 2% fat	0.12	3.4	42	85	127	169	212	254
cream cheese	0.11	3.0	47	93	140	186	233	279
gouda	0.20	5.5	25	51	76	102	127	153
muenster	0.18	5.0	28	56	83	111	139	167
muenster, "lite"	0.19	5.4	26	51	77	103	129	154
monterey jack	0.18	5.1	27	55	82	109	137	164
monterey jack, "lite"	0.18	4.9	28	57	85	113	142	170
mozzarella	0.16	4.4	32	64	95	127	159	191
mozzarella, "lite"	0.20	5.5	26	51	77	103	128	154
mozzarella, part skim	0.19	5.4	26	52	78	104	130	156
Parmesan	0.27	7.5	19	37	56	75	93	112
ricotta	0.10	2.9	48	97	145	194	242	290
ricotta, "lite"	0.13	3.7	38	75	113	150	188	225
ricotta, part skim	0.13	3.6	39	78	117	157	196	235
Swiss	0.21	5.8	24	49	73	97	122	146
Swiss, "lite"	0.21	5.9	24	48	71	95	119	143

TAG FACTORS—FOOD WEIGHTS TO TAG
Meat Group—Chicken

Chicken	TAG/ gram	TAG/ oz.	Grams of Food Equal to TAG					
			5	10	15	20	25	30
breast, fried	0.20	5.7	25	50	75	100	125	149
frank	0.16	4.6	31	61	92	123	153	184
liver	0.16	4.5	32	64	96	128	160	192
salad	0.11	3.1	45	91	136	181	227	272
dark, no skin	0.17	4.8	30	59	89	119	148	178
leg, fried	0.19	5.4	27	54	81	107	134	161
light, no skin	0.18	5.3	27	54	82	109	136	163
wing, fried	0.21	6.0	24	48	72	96	120	144

Meat Group—Duck

Duck	TAG/ gram	TAG/ oz.	Grams of Food Equal to TAG					
			5	10	15	20	25	30
roast, no skin	0.15	4.2	34	68	102	136	169	203
roasted, with skin	0.14	4.0	36	72	108	144	180	216

Meat Group—Eggs

Eggs	TAG/ gram	TAG/ oz.	Grams of Food Equal to TAG					
			5	10	15	20	25	30
Egg Beaters	0.08	2.1	67	134	201	268	335	402
eggs, boiled	0.10	2.7	53	106	158	211	264	317
eggs, fried	0.10	2.7	51	103	154	206	257	309
eggs, poached	0.09	2.6	53	107	160	213	267	320
eggs, scrambled	0.10	2.9	49	97	146	195	243	292
scramblers	0.12	3.3	43	87	130	174	217	261

TAG FACTORS—FOOD WEIGHTS TO TAG
Meat Group—Fish

Fish	TAG/ gram	TAG/ oz.	Grams of Food Equal to TAG					
			5	10	15	20	25	30
catfish, raw	0.11	3.0	48	95	143	190	238	285
crab cake	0.13	3.7	27	55	82	110	137	165
crab, steamed	0.12	3.4	42	84	126	168	210	252
fishsticks	0.17	4.9	29	59	88	118	147	176
haddock, fried	0.20	5.6	25	51	76	102	127	152
haddock, broiled	0.14	4.0	35	71	106	142	177	212
halibut, fried	0.21	6.0	24	48	72	96	120	144
halibut, broiled	0.16	4.5	32	63	95	127	158	190
oysters, fried	0.18	5.1	28	56	84	111	139	167
oysters, canned	0.08	2.4	60	121	181	242	302	363
perch	0.11	3.3	44	88	132	175	219	263
red snapper	0.12	3.3	43	86	130	173	216	259
salmon, Atlantic	0.14	4.1	35	69	104	139	174	208
salmon, pink	0.12	3.4	42	84	125	167	209	251
scallops, fried	0.22	6.2	23	46	69	92	115	138
scallops, steamed	0.15	4.4	32	65	97	130	162	195
shrimp in shell	0.08	2.4	60	120	180	240	300	360
shrimp, fried	0.25	7.2	20	40	60	80	99	119
shrimp, steamed	0.15	4.4	32	65	97	130	162	195
tuna salad	0.13	3.7	38	77	115	154	192	230
tuna, oil-packed	0.18	5.1	28	57	85	113	141	170
tuna, water-packed	0.16	4.5	32	64	95	127	159	191

TAG FACTORS—FOOD WEIGHTS TO TAG
Meat Group—Lamb

| Lamb | TAG/ gram | TAG/ oz. | Grams of Food Equal to TAG | | | | | |
			5	10	15	20	25	30
blade, roast	0.17	4.8	30	60	89	119	149	179
leg-serloin	0.18	5.3	27	54	81	109	136	163
loin chop	0.18	5.2	27	55	82	109	136	164

Meat Group—Nuts

| Nuts | TAG/ gram | TAG/ oz. | Grams of Food Equal to TAG | | | | | |
			5	10	15	20	25	30
almonds	0.35	10.6	14	28	42	56	70	84
Brazil nuts	0.27	8.0	19	38	57	76	95	113
cashews	0.44	13.2	11	23	34	45	57	68
hazelnuts	0.33	9.8	15	30	46	61	76	91
peanut butter	0.42	12.6	12	24	36	48	60	72
peanuts	0.42	12.6	12	25	37	49	62	74
peanuts in shell	0.28	7.9	18	36	54	71	89	107
pecans	0.26	7.8	19	38	58	77	96	115
sunflower seeds	0.29	8.2	17	34	51	68	85	102
sunflower seeds in hulls	0.21	5.9	24	48	72	96	120	144
walnuts	0.31	9.2	16	33	49	65	81	98

Meat Group—Pork

| Pork | TAG/ gram | TAG/ oz. | Grams of Food Equal to TAG | | | | | |
			5	10	15	20	25	30
Bac-o-bits	0.52	15.7	10	19	29	38	48	57
bacon, Canadian	0.15	3.8	34	68	102	136	170	204
bacon, fried	0.23	7.0	21	42	62	83	104	125

TAG FACTORS—FOOD WEIGHTS TO TAG
Meat Group—Pork

Pork	TAG/ gram	TAG/ oz.	Grams of Food Equal to TAG					
			5	10	15	20	25	30
bologna	0.11	3.1	45	91	136	181	226	272
ham, 5% fat	0.13	3.6	39	79	118	158	197	237
ham, 11% fat	0.14	4.0	36	71	107	143	178	214
pepperoni	0.14	3.8	37	73	110	147	183	220
picnic ham	0.20	5.7	25	50	75	100	125	150
pork chop, lean	0.21	6.0	24	47	71	94	118	142
potted meats	0.12	3.4	41	83	124	166	207	248
salami	0.14	3.8	37	73	110	147	183	220
sausage, pork	0.12	3.3	42	85	127	169	212	254

Meat Group—Turkey

Turkey	TAG/ gram	TAG/ oz.	Grams of Food Equal to TAG					
			5	10	15	20	25	30
dark, no skin	0.17	4.9	29	58	87	116	144	173
dark with skin	0.17	4.9	29	58	88	117	146	175
light, no skin	0.18	5.1	28	57	85	113	142	170
light with skin	0.17	5.0	29	57	86	115	144	172
turkey frank	0.11	3.0	47	94	141	189	236	283

Meat Group—Veal

Veal	TAG/ gram	TAG/ oz.	Grams of Food Equal to TAG					
			5	10	15	20	25	30
cutlet, fried	0.19	5.5	26	52	77	103	129	155
sirloin, braised	0.19	5.5	26	51	77	103	129	154

TAG FACTORS—FOOD WEIGHTS TO TAG
Milk Group

Milk	TAG/ gram	TAG/ oz.	Grams of Food Equal to TAG					
			5	10	15	20	25	30
2%-fat milk	0.07	2.0	72	145	217	289	362	434
buttermilk	0.07	1.9	74	147	221	295	369	442
Cambridge diet	0.64	18.4	8	16	23	31	39	47
chocolate 2% fat	0.12	3.5	40	80	120	161	201	241
eggnog	0.17	4.7	30	61	91	121	151	182
evaporated milk	0.16	4.4	32	64	96	128	160	192
malted milk	0.13	3.6	39	78	117	157	196	235
nonfat dry milk	0.73	19.9	7	14	21	27	34	41
skim milk	0.07	1.9	74	148	223	297	371	445
whole milk	0.07	2.0	72	143	215	287	359	430
yogurt, fruit	0.21	6.0	24	48	71	95	119	143
yogurt, plain	0.10	2.9	49	98	147	195	244	293

Starch Group—Breads

Breads	TAG/ gram	TAG/ oz.	Grams of Food Equal to TAG					
			5	10	15	20	25	30
bagel	0.63	18.2	8	16	24	32	40	48
biscuits	0.52	15.2	10	19	29	39	48	58
bread crumbs	0.81	23.0	6	12	18	25	31	37
bread, "lite"	0.42	11.5	12	24	36	48	60	72
breadsticks	0.82	24.5	6	12	18	24	30	37
cornbread	0.34	9.6	15	29	44	59	73	88
doughnuts	0.44	12.0	11	23	34	45	57	68
French bread	0.56	15.7	9	18	27	35	44	53
French toast	0.33	9.2	15	31	46	61	77	92
hamburger bun	0.56	15.9	9	18	27	36	45	54

TAG FACTORS—FOOD WEIGHTS TO TAG
Starch Group—Breads

Breads	TAG/ gram	TAG/ oz.	Grams of Food Equal to TAG					
			5	10	15	20	25	30
hot-dog bun	0.53	14.9	9	19	28	38	47	57
muffins								
blueberry	0.53	15.2	10	20	30	39	49	59
bran	0.48	13.6	11	21	32	42	53	63
English	0.51	14.5	10	20	30	39	49	59
pancakes/								
waffles	0.39	10.9	13	26	39	51	64	77
pizza crust	0.51	14.6	10	20	29	39	49	59
rolls	0.60	16.9	8	17	25	33	41	50
rye bread	0.53	14.8	9	19	28	38	47	56
sourdough								
bread	0.53	14.9	9	19	28	38	47	56
sweet roll	0.55	15.9	9	18	27	36	45	54
taco shell	0.73	20.0	7	14	21	28	34	41
tortilla, corn	0.47	12.8	11	21	32	42	53	64
tortilla, flour	0.63	17.2	8	16	24	32	40	48
white, roll	0.56	16.0	9	18	27	36	45	54
whole-wheat								
bread	0.54	15.6	9	18	28	37	46	55

Starch Group—Cereals

Cereal	TAG/ gram	TAG/ oz.	Grams of Food Equal to TAG					
			5	10	15	20	25	30
All-Bran	0.47	13.7	11	21	32	43	53	64
All-Bran,								
extra fiber	0.39	10.8	13	26	39	52	65	77
Bran Chex	0.87	24.4	6	11	17	23	29	34
bran flakes	0.87	24.4	6	11	17	23	29	34
bran, 100%	0.82	22.9	6	12	18	24	31	37
Cheerios	0.80	22.3	6	13	19	25	31	38
corn bran	0.90	25.1	6	11	17	22	28	33

TAG FACTORS—FOOD WEIGHTS TO TAG
Starch Group—Cereals

Cereal	TAG/ gram	TAG/ oz.	Grams of Food Equal to TAG					
			5	10	15	20	25	30
Corn Chex	0.93	26.1	5	11	16	21	27	32
cornflakes	0.91	25.6	5	11	16	22	27	33
Cream of Wheat	0.12	3.4	42	83	125	167	209	250
Fruit & Fibre	0.84	23.6	6	12	18	24	30	36
granola	0.75	21.1	7	13	20	27	33	40
Grape-Nuts	0.90	25.1	6	11	17	22	28	33
Most	0.86	24.0	6	12	18	23	29	35
oat flakes	0.84	23.6	6	12	18	24	30	36
oatmeal, cooked	0.12	3.5	40	81	121	161	202	242
oatmeal, dry	0.78	21.8	6	13	19	26	32	38
Product 19	0.90	25.1	6	11	17	22	28	33
Raisin Bran	0.87	25.5	6	11	17	23	29	34
Rice Krispies	0.93	25.9	5	11	16	22	27	32
shredded wheat	0.88	24.5	6	11	17	23	29	34
Special K	0.88	24.6	6	11	17	23	29	34
Total	0.86	24.0	6	12	18	23	29	35
wheat germ	0.55	15.5	9	18	27	36	45	54
Wheaties	0.86	24.2	6	12	17	23	29	35

Starch Group—Crackers

Crackers	TAG/ gram	TAG/ oz.	Grams of Food Equal to TAG					
			5	10	15	20	25	30
cheese crackers	0.61	18.2	8	16	25	33	41	49
graham crackers	0.79	22.2	6	13	19	25	32	38
Hi-Ho	0.66	17.7	8	15	23	30	38	45
melba toast	0.75	30.0	7	13	20	27	33	40

TAG FACTORS—FOOD WEIGHTS TO TAG
Starch Group—Crackers

Crackers	TAG/ gram	TAG/ oz.	Grams of Food Equal to TAG 5	10	15	20	25	30
saltines	0.83	25.0	6	12	18	24	30	36
Wheat Thins	0.77	27.0	6	13	19	26	32	39

Starch Group—Grains

Grain	TAG/ gram	TAG/ oz.	Grams of Food Equal to TAG 5	10	15	20	25	30
barley	0.84	23.9	6	12	18	24	30	36
grits, cooked	0.14	3.9	36	72	108	145	181	217
grits, dry	0.83	22.6	6	12	18	24	30	36
rice, brown, cooked	0.27	7.6	19	37	56	74	93	111
rice, dry	0.85	23.9	6	12	18	23	29	35
rice, white, cooked	0.25	7.2	20	39	59	79	99	118

Starch Group—Pasta

Pasta	TAG/ gram	TAG/ oz.	Grams of Food Equal to TAG 5	10	15	20	25	30
macaroni and cheese	0.37	10.6	13	27	40	54	67	81
noodles, cooked	0.25	7.0	20	41	61	82	102	123
pasta, dry	0.85	23.9	6	12	18	23	29	35
spaghetti, cooked	0.33	9.5	15	30	45	60	76	91

TAG FACTORS—FOOD WEIGHTS TO TAG
Starch Group—Snacks

Snack	TAG/ gram	TAG/ oz.	Grams of Food Equal to TAG					
			5	10	15	20	25	30
corn chips	0.72	20.1	7	14	21	28	35	42
granola bar	0.74	22.3	7	14	20	27	34	41
peanut butter and cheese crackers	0.61	16.9	8	17	25	33	41	50
pizza, cheese	0.34	9.7	15	29	44	58	73	87
pizza, meat	0.27	7.8	18	37	55	73	91	110
popcorn, no butter	0.84	23.6	6	12	18	24	30	36
potato chips	0.66	18.4	8	15	23	30	38	46
pretzels	0.86	24.0	6	12	17	23	29	35

Starch Group—Soup

Soup	TAG/ gram	TAG/ oz.	Grams of Food Equal to TAG					
			5	10	15	20	25	30
asparagus	0.05	1.4	98	196	294	392	490	588
bean with bacon	0.11	3.1	45	90	136	181	226	271
beef broth	Free							
black bean	0.09	2.7	53	106	160	213	266	319
chicken broth	0.02	0.5	314	629	943			
chicken chunky	0.10	2.9	50	99	149	198	248	297
chicken noodle	0.05	1.4	101	201	302	403	503	604
chicken and rice	0.04	1.1	128	256	384	512	640	768
chili con carne	0.17	4.9	29	58	87	116	146	175
lentil with ham	0.10	3.0	48	96	144	192	240	288

TAG FACTORS—FOOD WEIGHTS TO TAG
Starch Group—Soup

Soup	TAG/ gram	TAG/ oz.	Grams of Food Equal to TAG					
			5	10	15	20	25	30
mushroom/ milk	0.08	2.3	62	125	187	249	312	374
mushroom/ water	0.05	1.3	106	212	317	423	529	635
oyster/milk	0.02	0.7	211	423	634	846		
pea with milk	0.16	4.5	32	63	95	126	158	190
pea with water	0.13	3.6	39	79	118	157	197	236
spaghetti and meat sauce	0.17	4.7	30	60	90	120	149	179
tomato with milk	0.11	3.0	47	94	141	188	235	281
tomato with water	0.07	2.1	68	135	203	271	339	406
turkey vegetable	0.04	1.3	113	225	338	451	563	676
vegetable beef	0.06	1.6	89	179	268	358	447	537
vegetable beef stew	0.11	3.2	45	89	134	178	223	268
vegetable, chunky	0.09	2.5	56	112	168	224	280	336
vegetarian vegetable	0.06	1.6	80	159	239	319	399	478

Starch Group—Fruit

Fruit	TAG/ gram	TAG/ oz.	Grams of Food Equal to TAG					
			5	10	15	20	25	30
apple	0.15	4.1	34	68	102	136	171	205
apple with core	0.11	3.2	45	90	135	180	225	270
applesauce	0.11	3.1	46	92	138	184	231	277

TAG FACTORS—FOOD WEIGHTS TO TAG
Starch Group—Fruit

Fruit	TAG/ gram	TAG/ oz.	5	10	15	20	25	30
			Grams of Food Equal to TAG					
apricots	0.12	3.4	42	83	125	167	208	250
apricots, dry	0.64	18.7	8	16	23	31	39	47
banana	0.24	6.9	21	42	62	83	104	125
banana with peel	0.15	4.3	32	64	96	128	160	192
blackberries	0.13	3.7	38	76	113	151	189	227
blueberries	0.15	4.1	34	69	103	137	171	206
cantaloupe	0.09	2.6	56	112	168	225	281	337
cantaloupe with skin	0.04	1.1	126	253	379	506	632	759
cherries	0.17	4.9	29	58	87	115	144	173
cherries with stone	0.13	3.7	36	72	109	145	181	217
cranberries	0.13	3.8	38	77	115	154	192	231
cranberry sauce	0.39	11.2	13	26	39	51	64	77
currants	0.76	21.6	7	13	20	26	33	39
dates	0.73	20.8	7	14	21	28	34	41
dates with pit	0.65	18.2	8	15	23	31	39	46
elderberries	0.19	5.4	27	53	80	106	133	159
figs	0.19	5.3	25	51	76	102	127	152
fruit cocktail	0.12	3.4	41	82	124	165	206	247
gooseberries	0.11	3.0	46	93	139	186	232	279
grapefruit	0.08	2.3	62	124	186	248	310	372
grapefruit with skin	0.05	1.5	94	187	281	374	468	561
grapes	0.17	4.8	30	59	89	119	149	178
honeydew melon	0.10	2.7	53	106	159	211	264	317
kiwifruit	0.16	4.4	32	64	97	129	161	193
mango	0.17	4.9	29	58	86	115	144	173
nectarine	0.13	3.6	40	79	119	158	198	237

TAG FACTORS—FOOD WEIGHTS TO TAG
Starch Group—Fruit

Fruit	TAG/ gram	TAG/ oz.	Grams of Food Equal to TAG					
			5	10	15	20	25	30
orange	0.12	3.5	41	82	123	164	204	245
mandarin	0.10	2.8	50	100	150	201	251	301
navel with skin	0.09	2.6	55	109	164	219	273	328
valencia with skin	0.14	4.1	51	102	152	203	254	305
papaya	0.10	2.9	49	98	147	196	246	295
peach	0.11	3.1	43	86	130	173	216	259
peach with pit	0.10	2.7	53	106	159	211	264	317
peaches, canned	0.12	3.4	42	83	125	167	208	250
pear	0.15	4.4	33	65	98	130	163	195
pear with core	0.14	4.1	35	70	105	140	174	209
persimmons	0.34	9.7	15	29	44	59	73	88
pineapple, juice- packed	0.16	4.5	31	63	94	126	157	188
plum	0.14	3.9	37	74	111	148	185	222
plum with pit	0.12	3.3	30	61	91	122	152	182
prunes with pit	0.56	15.8	9	18	27	36	44	53
prunes, dry	0.62	17.4	8	16	24	32	40	48
raisins	0.79	22.5	6	13	19	25	32	38
raspberries	0.12	3.5	41	83	124	165	207	248
strawberries	0.07	2.0	67	134	202	269	336	403
tangelo	0.06	1.6	89	179	268	358	447	537
tangerine	0.12	3.2	43	87	130	173	216	260
tangerine with skin	0.09	2.6	56	112	168	224	280	336
watermelon	0.08	2.2	66	132	198	263	329	395
watermelon with skin	0.03	0.8	162	324	486	648	810	971

TAG FACTORS—FOOD WEIGHTS TO TAG
Starch Group—Fruit Juice

Fruit Juice	TAG/ gram	TAG/ oz.	Grams of Food Equal to TAG					
			5	10	15	20	25	30
apple juice	0.12	3.4	43	85	128	170	213	255
cranberry juice	0.15	4.2	33	67	100	134	167	201
grape juice	0.15	4.3	33	65	98	131	163	196
grapefruit juice	0.10	2.7	52	104	156	208	260	312
lime juice	0.08	3.0	51	103	154	206	257	309
orange juice	0.10	2.9	49	98	147	196	245	294
orange/ grapefruit juice	0.11	3.0	47	94	141	188	235	282
pineapple juice	0.14	4.0	36	72	107	143	179	215
prune juice	0.18	5.1	28	56	84	112	140	168
tomato juice	0.05	1.3	109	218	328	437	546	655
V-8 juice	0.05	1.4	106	211	317	422	528	633

Starch Group—Vegetables

Vegetable	TAG/ gram	TAG/ oz.	Grams of Food Equal to TAG					
			5	10	15	20	25	30
artichoke	0.12	3.3	43	87	130	173	217	260
asparagus	0.05	1.4	102	204	306	408	511	613
avocado	0.10	2.8	51	101	152	202	253	304
avocado with seed	0.07	2.1	68	135	203	270	338	406
bean sprouts	0.05	1.5	96	191	287	383	479	574
beans and chili	0.20	5.7	25	50	75	100	125	150
beans, white, cooked	0.26	7.4	19	39	58	78	97	116
beets	0.07	1.9	74	149	223	297	371	446

TAG FACTORS—FOOD WEIGHTS TO TAG
Starch Group—Vegetables

Vegetable	TAG/ gram	TAG/ oz.	Grams of Food Equal to TAG					
			5	10	15	20	25	30
blackeye peas	0.23	6.5	22	44	65	87	109	131
broccoli	0.07	1.9	77	153	230	307	384	460
Brussels sprouts	0.09	2.5	56	113	169	225	282	338
cabbage	0.05	1.4	101	202	303	403	504	605
carrots, cooked	0.08	2.2	65	131	196	262	327	393
carrots, raw	0.10	3.0	48	97	145	193	241	290
cauliflower	0.07	1.9	74	147	221	295	368	442
celery, raw	0.04	1.2	112	223	335	446	558	669
chard, cooked	0.04	1.3	115	229	344	458	573	687
coleslaw	0.07	2.0	71	143	214	285	357	428
collards, cooked	0.07	1.9	77	153	230	306	383	460
corn on cob	0.13	3.8	38	75	113	150	188	226
corn, cooked	0.17	4.8	30	59	89	119	148	178
corn, creamed	0.20	5.6	25	51	76	101	127	152
cucumbers	0.04	1.1	125	250	375	500	625	750
eggplant, cooked	0.05	1.3	106	213	319	426	532	638
green beans	0.04	1.1	134	268	402	536	670	804
greens, mustard	0.05	1.5	94	188	282	376	470	564
kale, cooked	0.06	1.7	84	169	253	337	422	506
kidney beans	0.20	5.7	25	51	76	101	127	152
leeks	0.13	3.6	40	80	120	160	200	240
lentils, cooked	0.24	6.8	21	42	63	84	105	126
lettuce, iceberg	0.03	0.9	155	311	466	622	777	933
lima beans, baby	0.30	8.7	17	33	50	66	83	100

TAG FACTORS—FOOD WEIGHTS TO TAG
Starch Group—Vegetables

Vegetable	TAG/ gram	TAG/ oz.	5	10	15	20	25	30
lima beans	0.24	6.9	21	41	62	82	103	124
mixed vegetables	0.13	3.7	39	78	117	156	195	234
mushrooms, raw	0.06	1.7	83	166	249	332	416	499
okra, cooked	0.07	2.1	70	139	209	278	348	417
olives, black	0.06	1.6	90	179	269	358	448	538
olives, green	0.04	1.0	137	273	410	546	683	819
onions	0.10	2.7	52	104	157	209	261	313
parsnips	0.16	4.5	32	63	95	126	158	190
peas and carrots	0.10	2.8	52	103	155	206	258	309
peas, frozen	0.18	5.0	29	57	86	114	143	172
peppers, green	0.06	1.6	91	181	272	363	453	544
pickle relish	0.35	10.4	15	29	44	58	73	87
pickle, dill	0.03	0.7	190	381	571	762	952	1142
pickle, sweet	0.37	10.6	14	27	41	54	68	81
pimiento	0.06	1.8	78	157	235	314	392	471
pork and beans, canned	0.22	6.1	23	47	70	93	117	140
potatoes au gratin	0.17	4.7	30	60	91	121	151	181
baked	0.23	6.5	22	44	66	88	111	133
boiled	0.18	5.2	27	55	82	109	136	164
fries	0.26	7.3	19	39	58	78	97	117
frozen	0.26	7.3	19	39	58	78	97	117
mashed	0.14	4.0	36	72	108	143	179	215
salad	0.16	4.6	31	62	93	124	155	186
sweet	0.34	9.7	15	30	44	59	74	89
pumpkin	0.09	2.4	59	118	177	237	296	355

TAG FACTORS—FOOD WEIGHTS TO TAG

Starch Group—Vegetables

Vegetable	*TAG/ gram*	*TAG/ oz.*	*Grams of Food Equal to TAG* 5	*10*	*15*	*20*	*25*	*30*
radish	0.04	1.2	119	239	358	477	597	716
rhubarb, raw	0.06	1.6	92	183	275	366	458	549
rutabagas	0.09	2.5	57	115	172	229	286	344
salad, three bean	0.18	5.1	28	56	84	112	141	169
salad, tossed	0.04	1.2	116	232	348	463	579	695
sauerkraut	0.05	1.5	97	194	292	389	486	583
snow peas	0.13	3.6	39	79	118	158	197	237
soybeans	0.18	5.1	28	56	85	113	141	169
spinach, cooked	0.07	1.8	76	153	229	305	382	458
squash	0.05	1.4	103	206	309	413	516	619
tofu (soybean)	0.07	2.1	68	136	204	272	340	408
tomato paste	0.21	5.9	24	49	73	97	121	146
tomato sauce	0.08	2.3	62	124	186	247	309	371
tomatoes	0.05	1.5	93	187	280	373	467	560
tomatoes, canned	0.05	1.4	100	200	300	400	500	600
turnips, cooked	0.05	1.5	93	186	279	371	464	557
water chestnuts	0.19	5.4	26	53	79	195	131	158
zucchini	0.04	1.2	120	241	361	481	602	722

Sugar Group—Beverages

Beverage	*TAG/ gram*	*TAG/ oz.*	*Grams of Food Equal to TAG* 5	*10*	*15*	*20*	*25*	*30*
beer	0.04	1.1	126	251	377	502	628	753
beer, "lite"	0.04	1.0	139	278	416	555	694	833
coffee	Free							
coffee, decaf	Free							

TAG FACTORS—FOOD WEIGHTS TO TAG
Sugar Group—Beverages

Beverage	TAG/ gram	TAG/ oz.	Grams of Food Equal to TAG					
			5	10	15	20	25	30
Gatorade	0.05	1.3	110	219	329	438	548	657
whiskey	0.04	1.3	110					
Kool-Aid	0.10	3.0	48	96	144	192	240	288
lemonade	0.10	2.8	51	103	154	206	257	309
limeade	0.11	3.2	45	89	134	179	223	268
soda, diet	Free							
soda, sweet	0.10	2.8	50	100	150	200	250	300
tea	Free							
wine	0.04	1.2	119	237	356	474	593	712

Sugar Group—Candy

Candy	TAG/ gram	TAG/ oz.	Grams of Food Equal to TAG					
			5	10	15	20	25	30
Almond Joy	0.73	20.3	7	14	21	28	35	41
caramel	0.74	20.7	7	14	20	27	34	41
chewing gum	0.77	23.0	7	13	20	26	33	39
gum, chewing, diet	free							
chocolate candy	0.65	18.7	8	15	23	31	39	46
Fruit & Nut	0.65	18.3	8	15	23	31	38	46
hard candy	0.97	27.2	5	10	15	21	26	31
Kit Kat	0.66	19.2	8	15	23	30	38	46
Life Savers	0.97	24.3	5	10	15	21	26	31
M & M's, peanut	0.68	18.9	7	15	22	29	37	44
M & M, plain	0.75	21.1	7	13	20	27	33	40
marshmallow	0.79	21.0	6	13	19	25	32	38
Milky Way	0.76	21.7	7	13	20	26	33	39
Mounds	0.76	21.3	7	13	20	26	33	39

TAG FACTORS—FOOD WEIGHTS TO TAG
Sugar Group—Candy

Candy	TAG/ gram	TAG/ oz.	Grams of Food Equal to TAG					
			5	10	15	20	25	30
Nestle's Crunch	0.70	19.1	7	14	21	29	36	43
Snickers	0.66	18.9	8	15	23	30	38	45
3 Musketeers	0.79	22.2	6	13	19	26	32	38
Twix	0.35	10.1	14	29	43	57	71	86

Sugar Group—Cookies

Cookies	TAG/ gram	TAG/ oz.	Grams of Food Equal to TAG					
			5	10	15	20	25	30
Animal Crackers	0.84	23.4	6	12	18	24	30	36
chocolate chip	0.70	17.5	7	14	22	29	36	43
fig bar	0.79	22.0	6	13	19	25	32	38
oatmeal	0.73	22.0	7	14	21	27	34	41
sandwich	0.74	20.8	7	13	20	27	34	40
sugar-butter	0.73	20.9	7	14	20	27	34	41

Sugar Group—Desserts

Dessert	TAG/ gram	TAG/ oz.	Grams of Food Equal to TAG					
			5	10	15	20	25	30
cake								
angel food	0.64	18.3	8	16	23	31	39	47
devil's food	0.46	13.0	11	22	33	44	55	66
pound	0.53	15.2	9	19	28	38	47	56
yellow	0.57	16.4	9	18	26	35	44	53
frozen yogurt	0.20	5.8	25	49	74	98	123	147
gelatin	0.14	4.0	36	71	107	143	178	214
ice cream	0.27	7.6	19	37	56	74	93	111
ice cream, diabetic	0.24	6.9	21	41	62	82	103	123

TAG FACTORS—FOOD WEIGHTS TO TAG
Sugar Group—Desserts

Dessert	TAG/ gram	TAG/ oz.	Grams of Food Equal to TAG					
			5	10	15	20	25	30
ice milk	0.25	7.1	20	40	60	80	101	121
pie, apple	0.39	11.1	13	26	39	52	65	78
pie, pumpkin	0.37	10.6	14	27	41	54	68	81
sherbet	0.31	8.9	16	32	48	64	80	96
Twinkies	0.61	17.1	8	16	25	33	41	49
pudding								
sugarfree	0.11	3.1	46	93	139	186	232	278
tapioca	0.20	5.6	25	51	76	102	127	153
vanilla	0.23	6.5	22	44	66	88	110	132

Sugar Group—Miscellaneous

Miscellaneous	TAG/ gram	TAG/ oz.	Grams of Food Equal to TAG					
			5	10	15	20	25	30
apple butter	0.45	12.9	11	22	33	45	56	67
BBQ sauce	0.09	2.5	52	105	157	210	262	315
creamer, whip	0.16	4.4	31	62	93			
creamer,								
nondairy	0.60	12.0	8	16	24	33	41	49
Equal	Free							
honey	0.83	23.7	6	12	18	24	30	36
jam-jellies	0.72	20.4	7	14	21	28	35	42
jelly, low-cal	Free							
ketchup	0.27	8.0	19	38	56	75	94	113
mustard	0.08	2.0	57	115	172	229	287	344
sugar	0.99	28.5	5	10	15	20	25	30
sugar, brown	0.96	28.4	5	10	16	21	26	31
syrup,								
chocolate	0.61	17.0	8	17	25	33	41	50
syrup, "lite"	0.27	8.0	19	38	56	75	94	113
syrup,								
pancake	0.74	21.1	7	14	20	27	34	41
vinegar	Free							

TAG FACTORS—FOOD WEIGHTS TO TAG
Fat Group

Fat	TAG/ gram	TAG/ oz.	Grams of Food Equal to TAG ½	1	2	5
dressings						
Thousand						
Island	0.21	6.0	2	5	9	24
French	0.21	6.0	2	5	9	23
French,						
low-cal	0.23	6.0	2	4	9	22
Italian	0.13	3.6	4	8	15	38
gravies						
brown	0.14	4.0	4	7	14	36
milk	0.14	4.0	4	7	14	36
white sauce	0.13	3.6	4	8	15	39
spreads						
butter	0.09	2.6	6	12	23	59
butter,						
whipped	0.09	2.5	6	11	22	56
margarine	0.09	2.6	6	12	23	59
margarine,						
diet	0.09	2.8	8	17	33	83
mayonnaise	0.11	3.0	5	9	18	46
mayonnaise,						
diet	0.18	5.4	3	6	11	28
vegetable oil	0.10	2.9	5	10	20	50

Index